CONTENTS

Studying English or English Literature at GCSE will involve you in reading prose fiction; in other words, imaginative writing in the form of novels or short stories by major writers published both before and after 1900. You may come across prose fiction as part of coursework, or perhaps in the form of anthologies or pre-release material issued before the exam, or you may meet it in the exam itself.

The **National Curriculum** specifies that students develop the ability to:

- Extract meaning beyond the literal, explaining how choice of language and style affects implied and explicit meanings

- Analyse and discuss alternative interpretations, unfamiliar vocabulary, ambiguity and hidden meanings

- Analyse and engage with the ideas, themes and language in a text

- Understand characters' motivation, the development of plot and a text's overall impact

- Distinguish between the attitudes of characters and those of the author

As you see, this means developing your ability to understand and **analyse how different features of a text contribute to its meaning and impact**. This guide is divided into different sections which deal with these features:

What happens? – Story, Plot, Narrative Structure
What's it all about? – Theme
Who's telling the story? – Viewpoint & Voice
Who's the story about? – Character
Where does the story happen? – Setting
How's the story told? – Language & Style

You may feel that considering a text under different headings like Theme and Character is rather an artificial, misleading thing to do, implying these features are totally separate from each other. You would be right – we might be talking about the plot of a story, and find we are talking about character at the same time, because, after all, events in a plot happen as a result of characters' decisions and reveal what characters are like.

You may also be saying 'But I thought reading was meant to be enjoyable!' And of course, you're right again! To be honest, there is always a risk that studying texts for an exam may detract from your enjoyment of them. However, this doesn't have to be the case. It can depend on how you look at it. Ideally, **studying a text and understanding how it works can increase your enjoyment and appreciation**. I once heard a student say that even after studying a text for a year, she was 'still friends with it'. Hopefully, you may feel the same.

You may find it encouraging, amidst all the emphasis on exams, that the National Curriculum also expresses the hope that students will 'read widely and independently solely for enjoyment' so that they will become (or stay!) 'independent, responsive and enthusiastic readers'.

good Luck!

WHAT HAPPENS? – STORY, PLOT, NARRATIVE STRUCTURE

Stories and structure

The effect on the reader

Order and endings

A story is a series of events. When studying a story or novel, we need to be sure we have grasped the main events that take place. As well as this, we need to be aware of how the author has arranged or ordered those events for us and why. **Another word for the way the author arranges the events of a story is the plot.** As an author influences our experience of the events in the story and the meaning we make of them through this arrangement, we need to be aware of it and its effect on us.

KEY CONCEPTS

Fiction refers to events that are invented or imagined ✳

Prose is ordinary language (not metrical language as in verse) ✳

A story is a series of events ✳

A story is a series of events

The Wedge-Tailed Eagle

First, let's look at how stories consist of events. Here is a series of events that form the backbone of a story called *The Wedge-Tailed Eagle** by Geoffrey Dutton:

✻   The setting is the Australian outback in 1941 where an Air Force base has recently been established. The area is also the home to a breed of huge eagles, which a local farmer complains have been attacking his sheep.

✻   Two pilots plan to fight an aerial duel with an eagle in their biplanes. The duel takes place. Several attacks on the bird fail.

✻   Finally, the eagle is hit, loses a wing and crashes to the ground.

✻   The pilots land and find the dead bird. They feel ashamed of what they've done, bury the bird, and fly away just as the farmer drives up.

* From *Australian Stories of Today*; also in *Modern Short Stories*, ed. J. Hunter (Faber, 1964)

Narrative structure

Presenting the events like this brings out a pattern or structure in the way the story has been put together. This is sometimes called the narrative structure. In the example above, the story goes through certain stages:

- **Exposition** – we are told who is involved, where and when events happen

- **Complication** – the characters are faced with a conflict, problem or challenge; their lives are complicated in some way

- **Climax** – the tension is at its highest; matters come to a head

- **Resolution** – a solution is found for the problem; an ending is finally arrived at

DID YOU KNOW?
Doris Lessing's story, *Through the Tunnel** (1957), has a similar structure. A boy challenges himself to swim through an underwater rock tunnel. The tension mounts until he finally succeeds, and feels he has proved himself.

Many stories take this shape. So, in fact, do real-life situations. On a recent train journey, I overheard an argument between two groups of passengers. One party had reserved seats, but arrived to find their lives 'complicated' (to use the above terms) by the fact that there were other people occupying the seats, who refused to move. The tense situation was eventually defused when the ticket collector arrived. He restored the seats to their rightful occupants by finding places in another carriage for the other travellers. As they left, one of them tried to restore

* From *The Habit of Loving* (1957); also in *Short Stories of Our Time*, ed. D. Barnes (Harrap, 1963)

a cheerful atmosphere by remarking brightly 'It's all been resolved!' You'll notice his choice of words echoes the 'Resolution' of the narrative structure.

My story is 'true' in that I didn't deliberately invent any of it. The events actually happened (although no doubt each participant made a different story out of them on reaching their destinations – the borderline between truth and fiction may not be as clearcut as we think!). Dutton's story of the biplanes and the eagles, however, is fiction – it is invented. If you look back, you'll see it also follows this structure.

It's as well to remember that the model shouldn't be applied too rigidly. For example, the last two features may occur at the same time. Also, the 'solution' may not always be a comfortable one for the characters! (In Charlotte Perkins Gilman's story *Turned*,* for example, the unfaithful husband returns to find his wife has left him, and is living with the girl with whom he had been unfaithful!)

KEY CONCEPTS

* A narrative is a story or account of events, real or imagined

* Plot refers to the arrangement or ordering of the events in the story by the writer

* Structure refers to the way a text has been constructed

The effect on the reader

The events in Dutton's story have been arranged in a way that creates an effect of tension in the reader. It appeals to our wish to know what happens next. Will man and machine or bird win the battle? We read on to find out. This sense of uncertainty (even anxiety if we sympathise with a character) as to future events is called **suspense**.

---

* From *The Charlotte Perkins Gilman Reader*; ed. Anne J. Lane, (Women's Press, 1981)

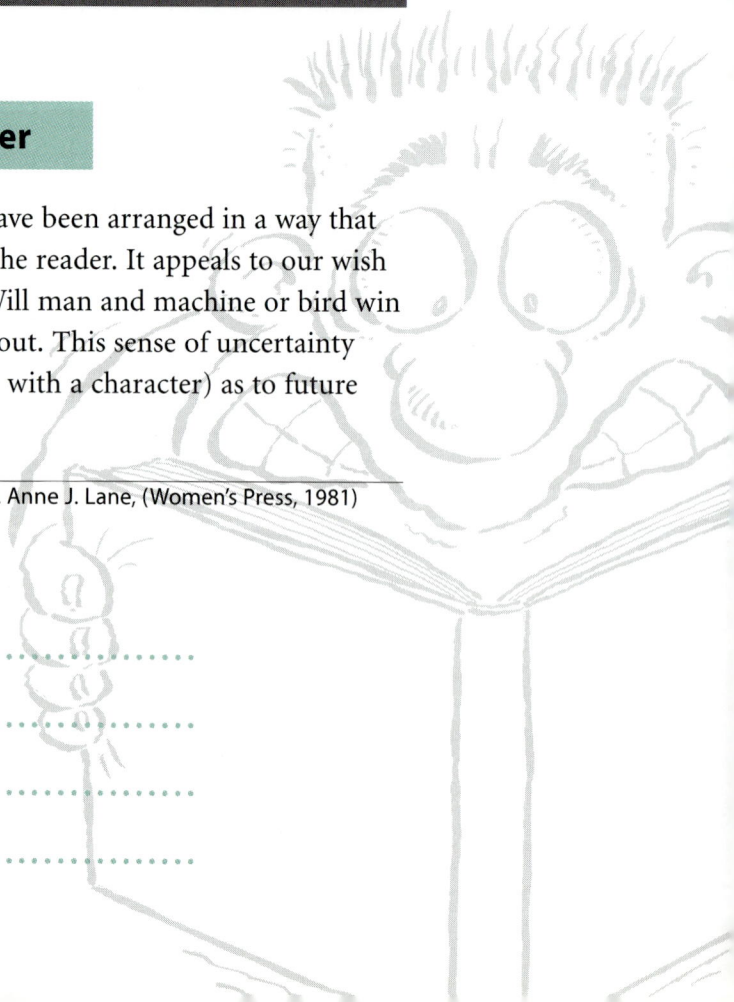

N
O
T
E
S

DID YOU KNOW?

In *The Arabian Nights*, Princess Scheherazade marries a king who has killed all his previous wives the morning after he married them. She escapes death by telling him stories, and breaking off at an interesting point just as the sun rises each morning. He spares her life as he wants to know what happens next.

And just then, there was a knock on the door...

Novels

Novels are longer and more complex than short stories, and may contain a number of climaxes. After having experienced the detail of a novel chapter by chapter, it's a good idea to stand back and look at its overall shape. Here, it may be helpful to consider a novel in the light of the structure we looked at above and see if it helps us grasp what's important.

Structure of *Lord of the Flies*

Lord of the Flies

If we try to identify elements of this structure, in William Golding's *Lord of the Flies* (1954) we might come up with something like this:

- **Exposition** – Some boys are marooned on an island with no adults, after their plane has been shot down in a war.

- **Complication –** A conflict develops. One group, led by Ralph, wants to live by rules and keep a signal fire lit in order to be rescued. Another group, led by Jack, becomes obsessed with hunting wild pigs. A further complication is that the boys come to believe there is a terrifying Beast on the island. Jack's group completely breaks away from Ralph's and turns into savages. They kill two of Ralph's remaining supporters, Simon and Piggy. Simon is killed, ironically, just as he comes to announce he has resolved the problem of the Beast by discovering it is only a dead parachutist. But the resolution he offers is ignored.

- **Climax –** Ralph, the only one who has not joined Jack's tribe of savages, is being hunted. As the hunters close in, Ralph falls.

- **Resolution –** Ralph looks up into the face of a naval officer who has just landed from a passing warship. The boys are rescued. This is only a 'happy' ending on the surface. The reader knows that if the naval officer hadn't arrived, Ralph would have been killed. Equally uncomfortable is the implication that as the adult rescuers are themselves engaged in a war, there is little to separate them from the children. The evil was not out there in the Beast, it is part of human nature.

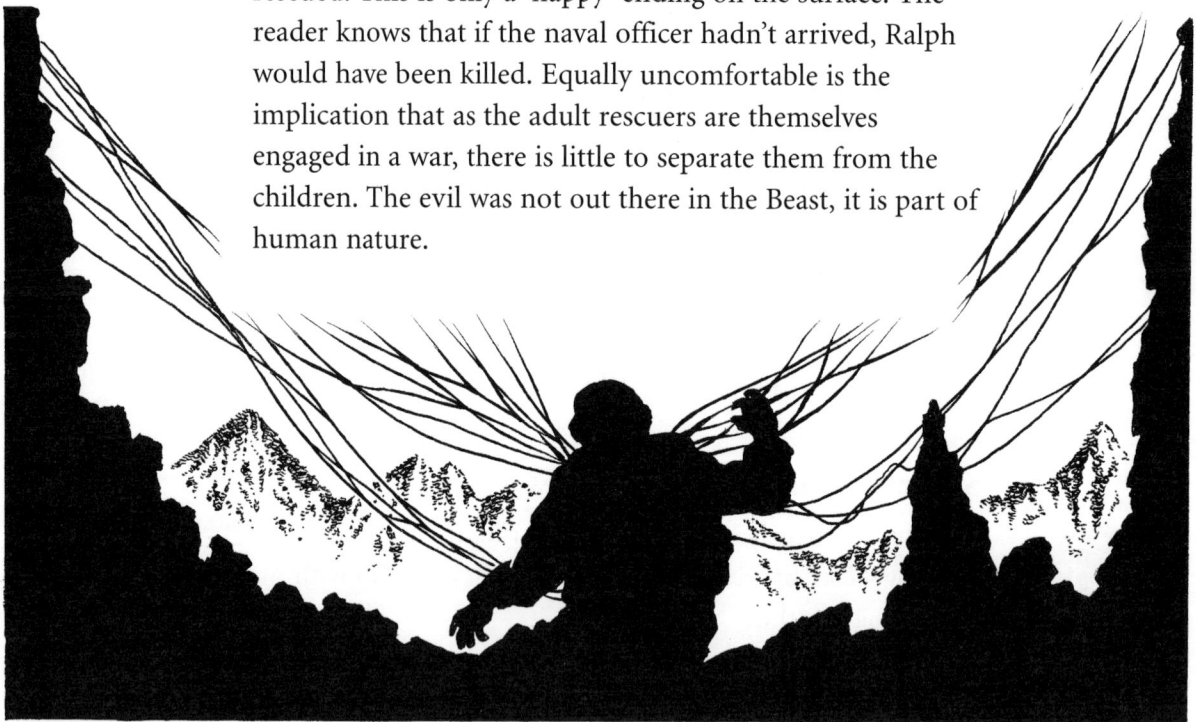

Those who have read the novel will know that this is only an outline. You'll be able to think of other climaxes that occur, such as the finding of the 'Beast' and the deaths of Simon and Piggy. **But seeing if you can identify elements of this narrative structure in a novel can help to highlight what's significant.**

In addition to looking at a novel from this point of view, it is worth remembering that each novel has its own shape.

Structure of *The Village by the Sea*

The Village by
the Sea

Anita Desai's *The Village by the Sea* (1982) is about an Indian boy and girl called Hari and Lila, who live in a country village called Thul, not far from Bombay. They are very poor; their mother is sick and their father drinks. Hari has been told by a stranger that a factory will be built there, which will change their lives but won't provide jobs for unskilled local people.

The novel falls into three main sections. Here is a brief summary that reflects none of the vivid detail in the book:

The village (Chapters 1–5). We are introduced to the family. A series of incidents, including the poisoning of their dog by one of their father's creditors, show the family's poverty and the bleakness of their future unless Hari can do something about it. He decides to go to Bombay to get work.

Bombay (Chapters 6–11). In the city Hari survives hardship and loneliness to find work in the kitchen of an eating-house, sleeping outside in a park. Later he is befriended by a watchmender, Mr Panwallah, who teaches him his skills as well as how to be adaptable and have confidence in himself.

Chapters in this section of the book repeatedly cut back to Lila in the village, showing her reaction to Hari's departure and how she is coping with the family and her mother's illness.

Hari hears on the radio of a huge storm in which local fishing boats have been lost. It reminds him of his ties with the village and he realises he must go home.

The village (Chapters 12–13). Hari returns with money, new skills, and plans to start a chicken farm. The younger members of the reunited family look as if they will be able to adapt successfully to future change.

If we stand back, we can see some distinctive features of the novel's structure – its division into three sections together with the cutting to and fro between Hari and Lila in the middle section. If we ask why the book has been structured in this way, it gives us an insight into the author's purpose and the book's themes ▶ **see pp 22–31**. The structure helps to convey such themes as the contrast between the country and the city, the importance of family ties, and the need to make choices and adapt when faced with change.

THINK ABOUT IT

Many nineteenth-century writers, like Charles Dickens, wrote their novels at first for monthly serialisation in magazines. The chapters were later bound together in complete volumes.

What effect on the writer's plotting do you think this form of publication might have?

Plots are not always arranged in chronological order

So far, we have looked at stories and novels in which the events are narrated in the order in which they would actually have occurred, in chronological order. However, this is not the only way of arranging events. **Writers may choose not to narrate events in chronological order.** Here is an example from Penelope Lively's story, *The Darkness Out There** (1980):

The Darkness Out There

* ✱ One summer day, a teenage girl goes to do odd jobs for an 'old dear' who lives alone in the country.

* ✱ On her way, she passes a dark wood which has a spooky reputation because during the war a German plane crashed there. Locals say the voices of the aircrew can sometimes still be heard. Her fear of the wood makes her think of other frightening things 'out there', like being attacked by gypsies.

* ✱ She arrives at the old woman's and does some jobs for her. She sympathises over the loss of the woman's husband in the war.

* ✱ The woman describes the night, years before, when the German plane crashed in the wood. She went out and found the crew, one of whom was still conscious, but injured and trapped. She left him there for two nights until he died, before reporting the crash.

* ✱ Appalled by the old woman's inhumanity, the girl leaves. She now realises that the 'darkness out there' that she feared is part of people, and that everything is not as it appears.

* From *Pack of Cards: Collected Short Stories* 1978–86; (Heinemann & Penguin, 1986 & 87)

HIGHER PERFORMANCE

In *The Art of Fiction* (1884), the novelist Henry James asked 'What is character but the determination of incident? What is incident but the illustration of character?'
What do you think he meant?

Here, if you look at the order in which events are narrated, you will see it is different from the order in which they occurred:

✳ The German plane crash and the old woman's discovery of the trapped airman happened before the opening of the narrative of the girl's visit as told to us.

✳ The author has arranged the plot so that the earlier events are kept from us until nearly the end, where they occur in what is called a **flashback**.

The use of this flashback technique produces a special effect: having from the start shared the girl's view of the spooky wood and the harmless old dear, we are made to share her changed view of the world and her shock as she discovers that the old dear is not as harmless as she appeared to be.

KEY CONCEPTS

✳ A flashback is a scene introduced to show events at an earlier time

✳ A climax is a point of the greatest intensity or interest

✳ Sympathy refers to the way we identify with, or share, a character's feelings

Wuthering Heights

This rearranging of events to achieve a particular effect on readers is often found in stories and novels. A famous example of a novel in which it occurs is Emily Brontë's *Wuthering Heights* (1847).

✶ We are introduced to the narrative in the year 1801 by a Mr Lockwood. He stays the night at Wuthering Heights where he reads a diary portraying events that happened back in 1777 to two characters, Heathcliff and Catherine. He falls asleep and has a terrifying nightmare. So intrigued is he by his experience, that when he returns to his lodgings, he gets his housekeeper, Nelly, to tell him the history of Heathcliff.

✶ We are then taken back in time to 1771 and shown how Heathcliff first arrived at the Heights, a ragged urchin from the Liverpool slums.

✶ The novel then alternates between the 'present' and the past in a series of flashbacks as Nelly satisfies Lockwood's curiosity by telling the history of Heathcliff's thwarted love.

✶ Finally, in the last few chapters, the plot moves forward from 1801 to 1802. Heathcliff dies and the next generation, on whom he has tried to avenge the loss of his love, overcome the past through their own love and are married.

The way the narrative structure of *Wuthering Heights* handles time can make it challenging to approach. However, Brontë's meticulous plotting is not done to deliberately confuse the reader. Through it, she achieves a number of effects. One of these is, by showing us a puzzling and extraordinary situation, to arouse our curiosity as to how this came about. Also, by going backwards and forwards in time, she is able to develop one of her themes, which is the powerful, potentially destructive effect of one generation on the next.

To sum up: There is a useful distinction between the series of events on which the story is based in the order in which they would historically have happened (the chronological order), and the way those events have been arranged and ordered by the writer (the narrative order). We need to be aware of what the important events are, and we also need to look at how the writer has arranged them and why.

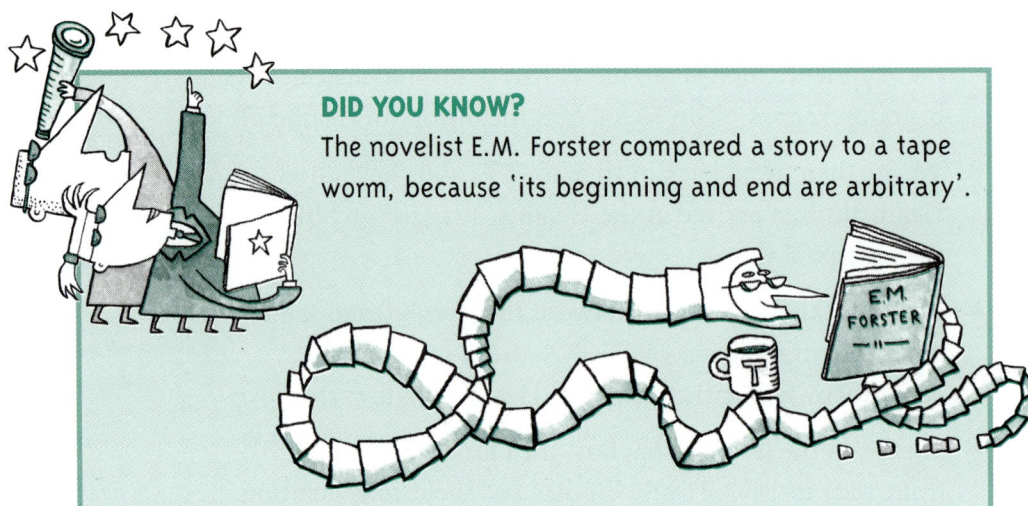

DID YOU KNOW?

The novelist E.M. Forster compared a story to a tape worm, because 'its beginning and end are arbitrary'.

Endings

There are many ways of ending a story. The ending may contain a twist or surprise, as in Penelope Lively's *The Darkness Out There*; or it may be expected, as in Guy de Maupassant's *Vendetta**, with its slow, relentless build up to the taking of revenge. It may involve characters facing the truth, as in Penelope Lively's story; or it may involve them running away from it, as in Patrick O'Brian's *Samphire***, where a husband refuses to believe his wife hates him enough to try to push him

---

*   From *Guy de Maupassant's Short Stories;* trans. M. Laurie (Everyman, 1934)
** From *Modern Short Stories;* ed. J. Hunter (Faber, 1964)

off a cliff. The reader may be left with the feeling that the matter is now closed, as in Geoffrey Dutton's *The Wedge-Tailed Eagle*; or be left wondering, as in Charles Dickens's *The Signalman**, where the signalman's death leaves the narrator pondering whether things are always as scientifically explicable as he had thought. This last kind of ending is sometimes called an 'open' ending.

It is useful to look at the ending, and see how it relates to the rest of the story.

In retrospect, how has the author prepared us for the ending?

In Lively's *The Darkness Out There*, if we look back having read the story, there are hints (such as references to the woman's glinting eyes and her prying into the girl's private life) that the 'old poppet' may not be what the girl has been led to think. So, when the final sinister revelation comes, we acknowledge that, although it is a surprise, it is believable and fits what we've been told.

The same applies on a larger scale to novels. We need to look at what the ending does with the events and relationships that the plot's complications have presented to us. Does the ending perhaps throw light on them in some way? Perhaps it gives us a fresh way of seeing them? What does it leave us thinking and feeling?

THINK ABOUT IT

The Russian writer, Anton Chekhov (1860–1904) wrote in a letter 'My instinct tells me that at the end of a novel or a story I must artfully concentrate for the reader an impression of the entire work'.

What advice might a writer draw from this about how to end a novel or story?
What kind of ending might Chekhov have disapproved of?

---

* From *The Penguin Book of English Short Stories;* ed. C. Dolley (Penguin, 1967)

HIGHER PERFORMANCE

1 Raymond Chandler, author of thrillers and detective novels such as *Farewell, My Lovely* (1940) is supposed to have given this advice to writers:

'When in doubt have a man come through the door with a gun in his hand'.

Chandler's suggestion might not have been meant entirely seriously. Imagine Jane Austen taking his advice in a novel like *Sense and Sensibility* (1811)!

However, it draws attention to two ingredients of a good plot: surprise and suspense. An event like this is likely to arrest the reader's attention and make them want to find out what happens next. Consider the use of surprise and suspense in any book you're reading yourself.

2 The novels of Ivy Compton-Burnett (e.g. *Manservant and Maidservant*, 1947) also contain crime although her world of claustrophobic late-Victorian households is a very different one to Chandler's. In the following comment, she seems to belittle the importance of plot. Why do you think this might be?

'The plot is not very important to me, though a novel must have one of course. It's just a line to hang the washing on.'

Perhaps Compton-Burnett is playing down the importance of plot because she finds exploring characters and themes, such as the abuse of power in families, more interesting.

Quiz

1. What four-letter word is sometimes used to describe the arrangement or organisation of events in a story?

2. What is a 'narrative'?

3. What word is used to describe a sequence of events which are arranged in the order in which they took place in time?

4. What is a flashback? And what do you think a flashforward might be?

5. What is a point in a novel or story called where the tension reaches a peak?

6. What are the three elements often found in the structure of a novel or story?

7. What three main questions does this section suggest you ask yourself when studying a text?

Answers

1. Plot

2. A story or series of events which somebody thinks important enough to tell us.

3. Chronological.

4. A flashback is when an author takes us back in time to tell us about events that happened before the point where the narrative begins. A flashforward takes us temporarily into the future.

5. Climax.

6. Exposition, complication, resolution.

7. What happens? How has the author ordered or arranged the events in the story? What is the effect of this arrangement on me as a reader?

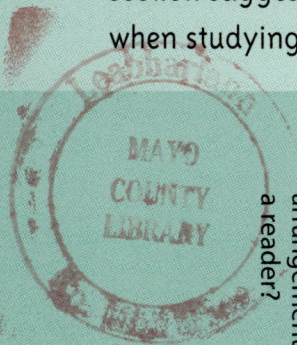

WHAT'S IT ALL ABOUT? – THEME

Making connections

Titles and narrators

Allegory

Studying a text is not just about looking at what happens.

It's also about making a meaning out of what we read.

So we need to do more than just retell the story, and say this happens, then that happens. Instead, we might say of a text that it deals with certain human experiences, ideas and concerns: love, guilt, revenge, racism, growing up and so on. Then we'd be talking about its themes.

KEY CONCEPTS

* Theme refers to the ideas, concerns and issues in a text

* A novel or story can have more than one theme

* Different themes may be noticed by different people

* Different themes may be noticed in different historical periods

A novel, as it is longer and more complex than a story, is likely to contain several themes. For example, the themes in Harper Lee's *To Kill a Mockingbird* (1960) include growing up, racism, and the dangers of judging by appearances. Those in Emily Brontë's *Wuthering Heights* include love, jealousy, loss, separation, revenge, violence, death and the supernatural, and the effect of one generation on the next, to name but a few!

DID YOU KNOW?

Wuthering Heights is an example of a novel that readers and critics have responded to very differently. Some have found it shocking and shapeless, others compare its vision and power to Shakespeare's. It's important to realise that alternative interpretations of a text are possible.

Reading may look like a passive way of passing the time, **but it's really an active process**. You make sense of a text by bringing to it all your own personal experiences along with all the things you've read. So it's not surprising that different readers notice different themes and it can enrich your experience of a text to exchange reactions to it with someone else. You can then make up your own mind – and, of course, you're perfectly entitled to change it in the future!

As we saw in the last section, one of the ways meaning is conveyed is through the way the events of the story are arranged and patterned by the author. **So, one way of identifying themes is to be on the look-out for patterns and connections.**

Making connections between events in the plot

Lord of the Flies

In William Golding's *Lord of the Flies*, we might start connecting events relating to the theme of how the boys, marooned on the island with no adults, become savages by gradually ridding themselves of the trappings of civilisation and respect for rules. We might notice the getting rid of clothes; the face-painting that removes inhibitions; the first killing of a pig and the chanting of 'Kill the pig. Cut her throat. Spill her blood'; the rejection of the rule that the person holding the conch shell should be listened to; the killing of Simon and Piggy and so on.

It's seeing connections that is important here, even between incidents that are widely separated. For example, in Chapter 4 Roger throws stones at younger children on the beach, but at that stage he daren't throw accurately enough to hit them because he is still influenced by 'parents and school and policemen and the law'. However, by Chapter 11, Roger's inhibitions have gone and he gleefully and deliberately pushes a huge rock which kills Piggy, the fat boy with glasses who has tried to insist on living by rules. Here the connection between the two incidents involving Roger shows how far he has descended into the savagery which is one of the book's themes.

You can read about other ways in which texts convey themes and meaning in the different sections of this guide. Let's look briefly at two additional ways in which stories and novels offer clues to interpretation, and help answer the question: **how do I identify a book's themes?**

What's in a title?

One clue to a book's theme can be the first thing that catches our eye: its title.

DID YOU KNOW?
The title of R.L. Stevenson's *The Strange Case of Dr Jekyll and Mr Hyde* (1886) about kindly Dr Jekyll inventing a drug that changes him into evil Mr Hyde, has become part of the English language. We talk about someone having a Jekyll and Hyde personality.

The first English novels, in the eighteenth century, tended to have the names of their central characters for titles, such as Daniel Defoe's *Robinson Crusoe* (1719), Henry Fielding's *Joseph Andrews* (1742) or Samuel Richardson's *Pamela* (1740-1). This is because early novels were influenced by the genres (the term for a kind or type of literature) of biography or autobiography.

KEY CONCEPTS

❋ Genre refers to a particular kind of literature

❋ Examples are science or romantic fiction; detective novels; thrillers

❋ Genre contain characteristic features which influence readers' expectations

Later, in the nineteenth century, writers sometimes used titles to draw attention to a theme, as in the case of Jane Austen's *Pride and Prejudice* (1813) or Charles Dickens's *Great Expectations* (1860–1):

* *Pride and Prejudice* refers to the Prejudice of the heroine, Elizabeth Bennett, and the Pride of the hero, Mr Darcy which keep them apart until they see behind their first impressions of each other.

* There are cases when an author's first ideas for a title are revealing. The first version of *Pride and Prejudice* was called *First Impressions*.

* The title of *Great Expectations* brings into focus the theme of how people have desires and 'expectations' based on illusions; in the case of the central character, Pip, this is of becoming a 'gentleman'.

DID YOU KNOW?

Novels with symbolic titles include D.H. Lawrence's *The Rainbow* (1915), where the rainbow suggests the idea of hope. In Joseph Conrad's *Heart of Darkness* (1902) and Penelope Lively's *The Darkness Out There*, the darkness represents the evil in humanity.

Some modern writers have chosen **titles containing symbols**. In Harper Lee's *To Kill a Mockingbird*, the mockingbird is an innocent songbird which the children are told it is a sin to shoot as it harms no-one. It becomes a symbol, associated with other characters in the book, in particular the black man Tom Robinson, shot trying to escape after being wrongly convicted of rape, and the recluse Boo Radley. These characters do no harm to anyone else, and the book claims it's just as much a sin to kill or persecute them as the mockingbird in the title.

Some writers may choose a **well-known quotation** as a title:

✳ Ernest Hemingway's *For Whom the Bell Tolls* (1940), a novel about the Spanish Civil War, is a quotation from a sermon by the seventeenth-century poet John Donne 'Any man's death diminishes me, because I am involved in mankind; and therefore never send to know for whom the bell tolls; it tolls for thee.' A whole view of war is implied by this title, if one knows the original reference.

✳ John Steinbeck's *Of Mice and Men* (1937), about the shattering of the dream of two migrant workers for a place of their own, is aptly titled if you know the lines from Robert Burns's poem 'The best laid schemes o' mice and men / Gang aft agley' (often go wrong).

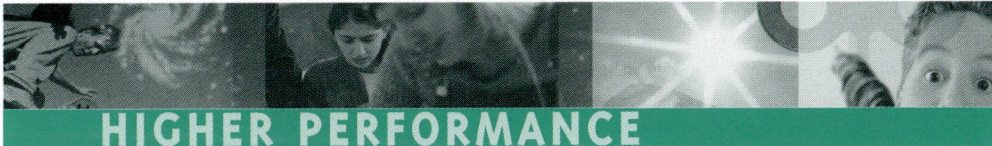

HIGHER PERFORMANCE

It's not only through its title that a text can take on meaning, but also through echoing or referring to another text. For example, Henry Fielding's *Joseph Andrews* (1742) parodies Samuel Richardson's *Pamela* (1740) and contains a scene based on the Good Samaritan parable. Jean Rhys's *Wide Sargasso Sea* (1966) draws on Charlotte Brontë's *Jane Eyre* (1847). This feature is called **intertextuality**.

Comments by the narrator

As well as titles offering a clue to a book's themes, **narrators may make explicit comments about key subjects and themes**. We don't necessarily have to believe these, and our experience of the book as a whole should be the basis for our interpretation, but they can be a useful starting point against which to test out our sense of what the book is about.

So, for example, in George Eliot's *The Mill on the Floss* (1860) the narrator justifies the time she has spent showing us the dull, narrow society in which bright young Maggie and her brother have to live:

I share with you this sense of oppressive narrowness; but it is necessary that we should feel it, if we care to understand how it acted on the lives of Tom and Maggie – how it has acted on young natures in many generations … that have risen above the mental level of the generation before them, to which they have been nevertheless tied by the strongest fibres of their hearts.

This, along with other similar comments, is a useful pointer to an important theme in the book: the effect on an intelligent, spirited individual of the limited society round her and the tragic conflict this causes.

Allegory

An allegory (derived from the Greek *allegoria*, speaking otherwise) is a story with a double meaning that can be interpreted on two levels, a surface meaning and a deeper meaning. John Bunyan's *Pilgrim's Progress* (1678) is an allegory of the Christian doctrine of salvation. On one level, it is about Christian, who, fleeing the City of Destruction, has various

adventures, encountering characters like Mr Worldly Wiseman and Giant Despair. He passes through places like the Slough of Despond (depression) and Vanity Fair (materialistic, worldly society) until he eventually arrives at the Heavenly City. On another level, it is about the experiences everyone faces on their journey through life.

Some people have seen *Lord of the Flies* as an allegory of the rise of fascism in Nazi Germany under Hitler (1933–45). They point to Jack's regimented choir with their black uniforms, the destruction of democratic institutions like the assembly and the conch, the eruption of violence and cruelty, and the killing of good people like Simon and Piggy. Whilst you may feel it limits the book to see its meaning entirely in this light, William Golding has said that his intentions in the book were didactic:

One of our faults is to believe that evil is somewhere else and inherent in another nation. My book was to say you think that now the war is over and an evil thing destroyed, you are safe because you are naturally kind and decent. But I know why the thing rose in Germany. I know it could happen in any country. It could happen here.

If you have enjoyed *Lord of the Flies*, or if you are interested in a novelist's comments on his own work, you may like to read the rest of Golding's essay, *Fable*, from which this extract comes (see *The Hot Gates*, 1965).

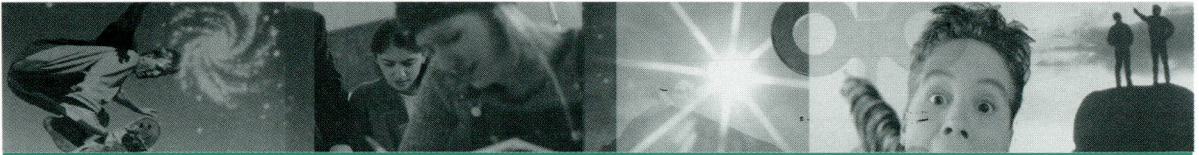

HIGHER PERFORMANCE

Here are two stories from *The Book of Mini-Sagas* (Alan Sutton Publishing, 1985), an anthology of stories written in just fifty words. Take each story individually and see if you can sum up its theme in a word or brief phrase. Then consider them together, and see if you can see any thematic connection between them.

Possessed by Love

Paulo loved his beautiful wife,
yet they quarrelled violently.
To see her flirting with
other men drove him mad. One
day he caught her with a
neighbour. 'My life is my own'
she cried – but Paulo killed her.
He could not distinguish
between what was proper and
what was property.

Brian Aldiss

What the Sleeping Beauty would have given her right arm for

This princess was different.
She was a brunette beauty with
a genius of a brain.
Refusing marriage, she
inherited all by primogenesis.
The country's economy
prospered under her rule.
When the handsome prince
came by on his white charger,
she bought it from him
and started her own
racehorse business.

Zoë Ellis

Quiz

1. What is the difference between plot and theme?

2. Can you think of examples of themes, other than those mentioned?

3. What does this section suggest are three possible ways into thinking about a text's themes?

4. Charles Dickens called some of his novels, like *Oliver Twist* (1837) and *David Copperfield* (1849–50), after the names of their central characters. Why do you think he didn't call *Great Expectations* after its central character?

5. Can you think of a story or novel, other than those mentioned, whose title suggests its theme?

6. Can you think of a text whose title is a quotation borrowed from another one?

Answers

1. Plot refers to the pattern of events; theme refers to a text's subject or meaning.

2. Any issue, concept, aspect of experience will do!

3. Looking for connections between events in the plot; thinking about the title; testing out comments by the narrator.

4. It wouldn't have drawn attention to his theme of people living by illusions.

5. How about Leo Tolstoy's *War and Peace* (1869)?

6. Aldous Huxley's *Brave New World* (1932) is a quotation (used ironically) from William Shakespeare's *The Tempest* (1611). William Thackeray's *Vanity Fair* (1847–8) is borrowed from John Bunyan's *Pilgrim's Progress.*

WHO'S TELLING THE STORY? – VIEWPOINT AND VOICE

Third person narrative

First person narrative

The 'unreliable narrator'

Viewpoint, or point of view, refers to the perspective the events in a story are being seen from. **Voice**, refers to the sense we may have, as we read, of someone who is speaking to us, telling the story. They are related, but different, because, as we shall see, we can hear a voice telling us a story, but the voice may be telling us what different characters are seeing and feeling.

KEY CONCEPTS

❋ Viewpoint is the perspective from which the story is told

❋ A narrator is the person telling the story

❋ An omniscient narrator knows everything

Viewpoint

Most stories and novels are told in either third person or first person narrative.

With third person narrative, the narrator refers to characters as 'he' or 'she' and shows us events from their viewpoint: 'She saw, felt or thought'. In first person narrative, events are seen from the perspective of the narrator: 'I saw, felt or thought'.

In his readable collection of articles The Art of Fiction (1992), David Lodge suggests: 'The choice of the point(s) of view from which the story is told is arguably the most important single decision that the novelist has to make …'.

DID YOU KNOW?

In one of *Aesop's Fables*, a man and lion argue over who is the stronger. They see a statue of a man strangling a lion. The man says it proves men are stronger. The lion objects: the sculptor was a man — a lion would have portrayed the lion strangling the man.

(Moral: How we interpret events is influenced by the person who shows us them)

Third person narrative – the omniscient narrator

An author may choose to have an 'omniscient' narrator who has an overall view of events. The narrator can comment on characters, and also move from inside one character to inside another at will, telling us their thoughts and feelings.

Charles Dickens uses an omniscient narrator in *Hard Times* (1854). This means he can give an overall view of working conditions during the industrial revolution. One chapter begins:

Hard Times

I entertain a weak idea that the English people are as hard-working as any people upon whom the sun shines. I acknowledge to this ridiculous idiosyncrasy, as the reason why I would give them a little more play.

In the hardest working part of Coketown; in the inner-most fortifications of that ugly citadel, where Nature was as strongly bricked out as killing airs and gases were bricked in … lived a certain Stephen Blackpool, forty years of age.

NOTES

At the same time, when he wants to, Dickens can get inside his characters' heads and show us things from their viewpoint.

In the extract below he presents the despair of Stephen Blackpool, who has been tied for nineteen years to an unfaithful, alcoholic wife, but wants to marry another woman, Rachael:

THINK ABOUT IT

In this extract from *Hard Times*, which words tell you that the viewpoint is that of Stephen?

O! Better to have no home in which to lay his head, than to have a home and dread to go to it, through such a cause. He ate and drank, for he was exhausted – but he little knew or cared what; and he wandered about in the chill rain, thinking and thinking, and brooding and brooding.

No word of a new marriage had ever passed between them; but Rachael had taken great pity on him years ago … and he knew very well that if he were free to ask her, she would take him. He thought of the home he might at that moment have been seeking with pleasure and pride.

NOTES

Elsewhere in the novel, Dickens uses other characters' viewpoints.

The blinkered Mr Gradgrind views the disastrous effects of his repressive child-rearing methods on his daughter, Louisa. When she collapses after confessing to an illicit extramarital relationship, 'he saw the pride of his heart and the triumph of his system, lying an insensible heap, at his feet'.
Next morning, we share Louisa's bewilderment:

....
Louisa awoke from a torpor, and her eyes … opened on her old bed at home, and her old room. It seemed, at first, as if all that had happened since the days when these objects were familiar to her were the shadows of a dream.
....

Why does Dickens choose omniscient narration in *Hard Times*?

- It enables him to give an overview of society, pointing out the destructive effect of certain ideas and practices in industry and education

- At the same time, he wants us to sympathise with the victims of these practices, such as Stephen and Louisa. Showing events from their viewpoint is a way of engaging the reader's sympathy with them

DID YOU KNOW?
Although the technique of omniscient narration is less popular now than in the eighteenth and nineteenth centuries, it is still alive and well. A contemporary writer from a very different culture, the Nigerian Chinua Achebe, uses it effectively in *Things Fall Apart* (1958) to show the tragic impact of white colonialism on tribal society. ▶ see p 48

Third person narrative – restricted viewpoint

The Village by the Sea

A writer may restrict the viewpoint to two characters or only one, depending on their purpose. In Anita Desai's *The Village by the Sea*, there is an alternation between two viewpoints, those of a brother and sister. Hari and Lila bear the whole burden of supporting their family, but Hari has been thinking of leaving his village and going to Bombay to find work:

Bombay! He stared out of the window at the stars that shone in the sky and wondered if the lights of the city could be as bright, or brighter. It was a rich city if he could get there, he might be able to make money, bring home riches, pieces of gold and silver with which to dazzle his sisters.

In the first half of Chapter 6, Hari has left his sister behind in the village and arrived in Bombay:

Hari stood watching the crowd fade away down the road. He felt deserted and friendless. … He belonged to no one, nowhere. The others had left him behind. He was alone in Bombay.

The viewpoint then switches to Lila, back in the village:

Waking up, she was aghast to see how bright it was. The white morning light was a shock, and so was … Hari's strange disappearance. She thought he must surely have come back in the night after walking off his anger but he was nowhere around.

This pattern of switching between two viewpoints continues during the central section of the book. With such a pattern, Desai brings out the contrast between city and country life, and shows the bond between brother and sister, engaging sympathy for them as they face challenges and choices during their separation.

Nineteen Eighty-Four

In George Orwell's *Nineteen Eighty-Four* (1949), the viewpoint is restricted to one character. Winston Smith is a secret rebel living under a dictatorship. He never knows who he can trust. Being restricted to Winston's viewpoint means we share his isolation and anxiety. Is the girl in the canteen who keeps looking at him a member of the Thought Police?

The sweat started out on Winston's backbone. A horrible pang of terror went through him. It was gone almost at once, but it left a sort of nagging uneasiness behind. Why was she watching him? Why did she keep following him about?

After the Thought Police catch him, we share his ignorance about his fate. At the chilling end of the book, we are enclosed within his thoughts when, after being tortured, he chooses to believe the Party is right in everything. He gazes up lovingly into a huge portrait of Big Brother:

Forty years it had taken him to learn what kind of smile was hidden beneath the dark moustache. O cruel needless misunderstanding! O stubborn, self-willed exile from the loving breast! Two gin-scented tears trickled down the sides of his nose. But it was all right, everything was all right, the struggle was finished. He had won the victory over himself. He loved Big Brother.

BIG BROTHER IS WATCHING YOU

First person narrative

The author may choose to invent a character and let them tell the story: 'This happened to me'.

In Harper Lee's *To Kill a Mockingbird*, we see the story from the viewpoint of Scout. As an adult, she looks back on her childhood:

When he was thirteen, my brother Jem got his arm badly broken at the elbow. When it healed, and Jem's fears of never being able to play football were assuaged, he was seldom self-conscious about his injury.

At times, we also share the viewpoint of the young Scout. Here she describes the night she and her brother Jem were attacked by an unknown assailant:

I ran in the direction of Jem's scream and sank into a flabby male stomach. Its owner said, 'Uff!' … His stomach was soft but his arms were like steel. He slowly squeezed the breath out of me. I could not move. Suddenly he was jerked backwards and flung on the ground.

Although these events are narrated from the adult perspective, we share the sensations of the young Scout together with her ignorance as to how her attacker was suddenly pulled off her.

DID YOU KNOW?
Charles Dickens's *Great Expectations* and L.P. Hartley's *The Go-Between* (1953) are also narrated by an adult looking back on their childhood. In each case, the experiences of childhood are vividly evoked, but we can also see how the adult telling the story has been affected by them.

Thinking about who is telling the story, and the point of view from which events are seen, can help us understand the author's purpose and fully appreciate the meaning of the text.

KEY CONCEPTS

✳ Voice describes the way we seem to hear the person who is telling the story

✳ Tone refers to the kind of voice we hear: e.g. angry, sympathetic

✳ Irony: the true meaning isn't the surface meaning

Voice

Take this description from the opening of George Orwell's *Nineteen Eighty-Four* (1949).

The hallway smelt of boiled cabbage and old rag mats. At one end of it a coloured poster, too large for indoor display, had been tacked to the wall. It depicted simply an enormous face, more than a metre wide the face of a man of about forty-five, with a heavy moustache and ruggedly handsome features.

The narrator's voice doesn't intrude very obviously here; **in third person narrative a story is often told in an impersonal way.** However, sometimes we get a strong sense of a voice telling the story. It might be angry or sympathetic; it might be terse or long-winded, witty or ironic.

THINK ABOUT IT

The distinction between the voice of the 'author' and that of an invented character isn't a clearcut one. Even when it seems to be the 'author' talking to us, the voice has still been constructed in words by the writer, for a particular effect.

NOTES

In first person narrative, the voice telling us the story is often that of a character invented by the author and given a name and a distinct language.

In *Paddy Clarke Ha Ha Ha* (1993), Roddy Doyle creates the character of Paddy with the voice and language of a child:

....

My ma saw us and she blabbed to my da. She was out on a walk with the girls and she saw us grabbing a pile of Woman's Ways. I saw her before I went down the lane. I pretended I didn't. My legs weren't there for a few seconds; my stomach felt empty and full; I had to stop a moan from getting out … I had to go to the toilet, immediately.

....

The use of words like 'blabbed', 'ma' and 'da', the short sentences and breathless rhythm create the distinctive voice of a child character separate from the author.

DID YOU KNOW?
Mark Twain claimed he took pains to create an authentic dialect voice for his young narrator in *Huckleberry Finn* (1885):

....

You don't know about me, without you have read a book by the name of The Adventures of Tom Sawyer, but that ain't no matter. That book was made by Mr Mark Twain, and he told the truth, mainly. There was things which he stretched, but mainly he told the truth.

....

Wuthering Heights

A very different voice greets us at the opening of Emily Brontë's *Wuthering Heights*, that of Mr Lockwood on his first visit to Heathcliff:

I would have made a few comments, and requested a short history of the place from the surly owner, but his attitude at the door appeared to demand my speedy entrance, or complete departure, and I had no desire to aggravate his impatience, previous to inspecting the penetralium.

The use of the long sentence and formal Latin-based vocabulary (and the Latin word penetralium meaning the inside of the house) makes Lockwood seem educated and civilised, but also rather pompous and affected.

Some readers are put off by Lockwood's voice, mistaking it for that of the author. But Brontë means us to be critical of Lockwood, even to laugh at his mistakes; his limitations as a narrator contribute to the novel as a whole.

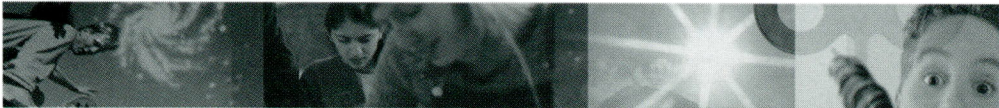

HIGHER PERFORMANCE

Wuthering Heights contains the voices of many narrators. At times, Lockwood tells us what his housekeeper Nelly has told him of what another character has told her! Notice the difference between Lockwood's voice (above) and the passionate voice of Heathcliff telling Nelly how he sensed Catherine's presence after her death:

I looked round impatiently – I felt her by me – I could almost see her, and yet I could not! I ought to have sweat blood then, from the anguish of my yearning – from the fervour of my supplications to have but one glimpse! I had not one.

The 'unreliable narrator'

The technique of the 'unreliable narrator' used by Emily Brontë is popular with modern writers. In Tom McAfee's story, *This is My Living Room* (1966), set in the American Deep South, the narrator expresses his views about life. However, it soon becomes clear that although he prides himself on his own integrity and reads a magazine called *Christian Living*, he is in fact violent, racist and sexist. When his wife doesn't want to learn how to shoot, he slaps her. He won't let his daughters date boys, but has a mistress himself. We can hear his contemptuous tone in his description of his wife:

Rosie ain't exactly good looking. She's got to be dried-up but once she was on the fat side. She makes a good wife. I've been married to her for going on thirty years. Sometimes I get fed up with her and go to my woman in South Town. I take her a couple of cans of beans and some hose or a pair of bloomers. There ain't nothing much a woman won't do for food or clothes.

We'd be misreading this story if we confused the narrator with the writer! The overall effect of the story is ironic, because the full truth of the situation is shared between the author and the reader, but hidden from the character telling the story.

Why is the question of narrative voice significant? Because it influences us. It guides us through the text, selecting, emphasising, commenting, inviting us to respond in particular ways. If we're aware of the voice, we can choose whether to respond in the way it invites us to, and understand a text's effect on us more fully.

HIGHER PERFORMANCE

In some of the above examples, the authors use a technique that brings us very close to the mind of the character. Although, in *Nineteen Eighty-Four* George Orwell writes in the third person 'Why was she watching him? Why did she keep following him about?', we can at the same time hear Winston saying to himself: 'Why is she watching me? Why does she keep following me about?" The same is true of Anita Desai when she writes of Hari: 'If he could get there, he might be able to make money'. If we change the pronoun 'he' to 'I', we have Hari's inner words or thoughts.

This technique of making the voice of the narrator merge with the words or thoughts of the character is sometimes called free indirect style. The thought or speech is indirect, because it is being reported, but it is free of a reporting clause, like 'She said to herself'. It enables us to share the character's thoughts and feeling more immediately, without the narrator getting in the way.

In this extract from Jane Austen's *Emma* (1816), Emma is reproving herself for her behaviour towards Harriet. Consider at what point you can hear the voice of the narrator starting to blend or overlap with that of the character, and what the effect of this is:

Her own conduct, as well as her own heart, was before her in the same few minutes. She saw it all with a clearness which had never blessed her before. How improperly had she been acting by Harriet! How inconsiderate, how indelicate, how irrational, how unfeeling had been her conduct! What blindness, what madness had led her on!

Quiz

1. What is meant by 'viewpoint' ?

2. What is meant by 'voice'?

3. Is it possible for the viewpoint to change within a text?

4. Why might an author write from the viewpoint of a particular character?

5. In Chinua Achebe's *Things Fall Apart*, set in nineteenth century Africa, Okonkwo is a leading warrior in his village. Ikemefuna is a boy hostage from a neighbouring tribe, who has been given by the village elders to Okonkwo to look after. After three years the boy regards Okonkwo as a father. One day, the elders decide Ikemefuna should be killed. Okonkwo is told that because of his closeness to the boy he shouldn't be involved. However, Okonkwo is afraid of appearing weak so he joins the execution party as it heads into the forest with Ikemefuna, who has been told he is going back to his village. From whose viewpoint do we see things in this extract? Is there more than one?

> *Ikemefuna felt like a child once more. It must be the thought of going home to his mother.*
>
> *One of the men behind him cleared his throat. Ikemefuna looked back, and the man growled at him to go on and not stand looking back. The way he said it sent cold fear down Ikemefuna's back. His hands trembled vaguely on the black pot he carried. Why had Okonkwo withdrawn to the rear? Ikemefuna felt his legs melting under him. And he was afraid to look back.*
>
> *As the man who had cleared his throat drew up and raised his machet, Okonkwo looked away. He heard the blow. The pot fell and broke in the sand. He heard Ikemefuna cry 'My father, they have killed me!' as he ran towards him. Dazed with fear, Okonkwo drew his machet and cut him down. He was afraid of being thought weak.*

Answers

1. 'Viewpoint' refers to the perspective from which the story is told.

2. 'Voice' refers to who is telling the story.

3. Yes. See *Hard Times* and *The Village by the Sea*.

4. To help us understand their feelings and motives; to engage our sympathy.

5. The viewpoints are those of Ikemefuna, then Okonkwo. Finally, the omniscient narrator explains Okonkwo's action.

WHO'S THE STORY ABOUT? – CHARACTER

Portraying characters

Understanding characters

Reacting to characters

One of our chief interests in a novel or story is the characters:

what they look like, what happens to them, their feelings and motives, whether they learn or change. We may also find ourselves reacting strongly to the characters: we may like or dislike them; feel critical or sympathetic towards them.

There are many different kinds of characters in novels and stories. For example, a character may have one or two qualities and not change throughout the book, or they may change in response to events and be capable of surprising us.

DID YOU KNOW?

Caricature is a term sometimes applied to drawing. In literature, it refers to the use of exaggeration to make a character look ridiculous. (They may have one or two prominent qualities like greed or snobbery.) The brutal Wackford Squeers in Charles Dickens's *Nicholas Nickleby* (1838–9) is an example.

There are also many different ways in which writers may present characters and influence our reactions to them. For example, a writer may introduce a character by describing their physical appearance, and add comments, for instance that the character is clever or proud. A writer may also reveal characters by showing their actions and speech, sometimes leaving us to draw our own conclusions about them.

KEY CONCEPTS

- A character's physical appearance can suggest their inner qualities ✳
- Characters are revealed by their actions and speech ✳
- Always consider what a character contributes to the text as a whole ✳

Methods of portraying characters

Nicholas Nickelby

Let's look at some of the methods used to portray characters in two very different examples. First, here is how Charles Dickens presents Wackford Squeers, in *Nicholas Nickleby*. Squeers is a brutal conman, caring only about making money out of the children he mistreats in his 'school'. He has only one eye:

Mr Squeers's appearance was not prepossessing. ... The eye he had was unquestionably useful, but decidedly not ornamental ... and in a shape resembling the fan-light of a street door. The blank side of his face was much wrinkled and puckered up, which gave him a very sinister appearance, especially when he smiled ... his expression bordered closely on the villainous. His hair was very flat and shiny, save at the ends, where it was brushed stiffly up from a low protruding forehead, which assorted well with his harsh voice and coarse manner. He ... wore ... a suit of scholastic black but ... he appeared ill at ease in his clothes, and as if he were in a perpetual state of astonishment at finding himself so respectable.

DID YOU KNOW?

In social comedy and satire, characters are sometimes suggested by their names. For example: Mrs Slipslop and Lady Booby (Henry Fielding); Lord Verisopht and Sir Mulberry Hawk (Charles Dickens); Fanny Throbbing and Walter Outrage (Evelyn Waugh).

In *Ways of Escape* (1981), Graham Greene writes: 'There is a magical quality in names – to change the name is to change the character'.

There are a lot of details we could dwell on here. To start with there is Squeers's name. 'Wackford' suggests his fondness for beating children, a brutality also implied by the 'low protruding forehead'; 'Squeers' is a distortion of the the word squire (meaning gentleman) which is what he is pretending to be but clearly isn't. The name also alludes to his queer (odd), lop-sided facial features, which Dickens uses to imply his twisted, lop-sided moral nature. **Dickens is using Squeers's external appearance to tell us about his inner qualities.** The way his eye is described using the image of 'the fanlight of a street door' makes it impossible for one to imagine it showing any human sympathy.

DID YOU KNOW?

Writers often use images and comparisons to suggest qualities in a character. At the start of *Of Mice and Men*, John Steinbeck suggests the size, strength and simplicity of Lennie by showing him 'dragging his feet a little, the way a bear drags his paws', and describing how he 'dabbled his big paw in the water' of the river.

Squeers's smarmed down hair and scholastic black suit suggest someone trying to impress, but the fact that the suit doesn't fit exposes the miserly fraud inside the clothes. Our view of Squeers is also influenced by the satirical tone of the narrator's voice, and by explicit comments like the reference to Squeers's 'villainous' expression.

Dickens goes on to develop our impression of Squeers through showing us his actions and letting us hear him speak. Squeers, in London looking for new pupils to take back to Yorkshire, is cross because so far he has only recruited three:

'At Midsummer,' muttered Mr Squeers ... 'I took down ten boys; ten twentys is two hundred pound. I go back at eight o'clock to-morrow morning, and have got only three – three oughts is an ought – three twos is six-sixty pound. What's come of all the boys? What's parents got in their heads? What does it all mean?'

Here, the little boy on top of the trunk gave a violent sneeze:

'Haoa, sir!' growled the schoolmaster, turning round. 'What's that, sir?'

'Nothing, please sir,' said the little boy.

'Nothing, sir!' exclaimed Squeers.

'Please sir, I sneezed,' rejoined the little boy, trembling till the little trunk shook under him.

'Oh! sneezed, did you?' retorted Mr Squeers. 'Then what did you say "nothing" for, sir?'

In default of a better answer to this question, the little boy screwed up a couple of knuckles into each of his eyes and began to cry, wherefore Mr Squeers knocked him off the trunk with a blow on one side of his face, and knocked him on again with a blow on the other.

A few moments later, a prospective parent enters. Squeers, pretending not to have noticed him, speaks to the child he has just bullied:

'My dear child,' said Mr Squeers, 'all people have their trials. ... You are leaving your friends, but you will have a father in me, my dear, and a mother in Mrs Squeers.'

The nauseating way Squeers shifts his style, calling the boy 'my dear' for the benefit of a customer shows his hypocrisy. Dickens reveals this, along with Squeers's brutality and concern with making money, through his actions and speech. Not surprisingly, we don't have any sympathy for Squeers. Dickens is using him in an attack on inhumane, badly run schools and on greed and inhumanity in society in general.

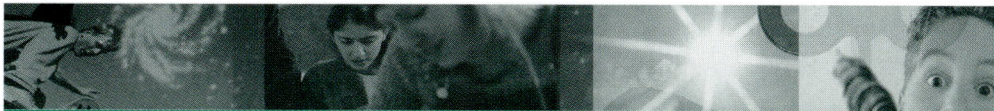

HIGHER PERFORMANCE

In *Aspects of the Novel* (1927), E.M. Forster distinguishes between 'flat' and 'round' characters. Flat characters 'are sometimes called types, and sometimes caricatures. ... They are not changed by circumstances'. Round characters, however, 'cannot be summed up in a single phrase' and are changed by the scenes they pass through.

So we can see how Dickens creates and influences our impression of Squeers through various methods:
- his name, and what it suggests
- details of physical appearance, including clothes
- Squeers's words and action
- the tone of voice in which the character is described
- explicit comment by the narrator (using words like 'villainous')

Characters who change and learn

There are many novels in which characters do change. Winston Smith in George Orwell's *Nineteen Eighty-Four* starts off as a secret rebel, critical of the Party and Big Brother, but, after months of brainwashing and torture, he gives up and accepts the Party is right. In Alice Walker's *The Color Purple* (1983), Celie starts off lacking self-confidence, oppressed by a husband who beats her; she is changed through her relationship with Shug Avery, learning to fight back and discover hidden strength and talents.

In studying novels like these, it's important to note the key experiences of the characters and how they are changed by or learn from these experiences.

KEY CONCEPTS

✳ Some characters in fiction learn and change

✳ We need to look at how characters are affected by their experience

✳ First and final impressions of a character are worth comparing

NOTES

Personal response

One thing you may be asked to write about after studying a novel is your response to the characters, and how the author has influenced that response.

There's little doubt that anyone reading *Nicholas Nickleby* will find Squeers highly repellent! And we can see how our response to him has been influenced by the narrator's comments and tone, by the choice of his name, and through the portrayal of his physical appearance, speech and actions.

Roll of Thunder, Hear My Cry

Let's look at a second example, from a modern novel also concerned with social wrongs. Mildred Taylor's *Roll of Thunder, Hear My Cry* (1976) uses some of the same methods as Charles Dickens (revealing character through speech and action) but in other respects, the approach and effect are different. It is written using a technique that engages our sympathy for one of the main characters, nine-year-old Cassie, because events are seen from her viewpoint ▶ **see pp 32–40.** As you will see, Taylor writes the novel using the technique of first person narrative. Cassie is the 'I' of the novel. So we are in a position to share Cassie's feelings as she learns, in a series of incidents, about the hardships and injustices experienced by blacks in Mississippi in the 1930s.

Cassie has a strong sense of right and wrong. She is an intelligent girl whose mother is a teacher, and having been brought up to respect herself, she doesn't understand, to start with, that Blacks are meant to adopt a subservient attitude to Whites. In one incident, Cassie and her brother, Stacey, are being served in a store in the nearby town of Strawberry, Mississippi, by the white storekeeper, Mr Barnett. However, when some white customers come into the store, Mr Barnett breaks off to serve them instead. We share Cassie's puzzlement as she tells us how Mr Barnett behaved 'as if we were not even there'. Cassie politely reminds him she was being served first. He ignores her, so she tugs his sleeve to get his attention. He recoils in horror, telling her to get her 'little black self over there and wait some more'. In her innocence, Cassie appeals to his sense of justice. We share her sense of shock at his response:

....

'We been waiting on you for near an hour,' I hissed, 'while you 'round here waiting on everybody else. And it ain't fair. You got no right –'
'Whose little nigger is this?' bellowed Mr Barnett.
Everybody in the store turned and stared at me. 'I ain't nobody's little nigger!' I screamed, angry and humiliated.

....

Mr Barnett turns on Cassie's elder brother, Stacey:

....

'She your sister, boy?' Mr Barnett spat across the counter.
Stacey bit his lower lip and gazed into Mr Barnett's eyes. 'Yessir.'
'Then you get her out of here,' he said with hateful force. 'And make sure she don't come back till yo' mammy teach her what she is.'

....

At this stage of the novel, Stacey is a contrast for Cassie, bringing out her innocence. He knows more than Cassie about a society in which the terrifying 'night riders' can take the law into their own hands to punish any blacks who step out of line.

DID YOU KNOW?
Contrast is a technique that makes one character's qualities stand out in relation to another's. In John Steinbeck's *Of Mice and Men*, Lennie's simplicity stands out against George's sharpness; in Alice Walker's *The Color Purple*, Celie's initial passivity contrasts with Shug's assertiveness.

So Stacey pushes Cassie out of the door to escape Mr Barnett's fury. 'What's the matter with you?' she asks. 'You know he was wrong!' She is so preoccupied with trying to understand Mr Barnett's behaviour that she accidentally bumps into a white girl on the sidewalk. She apologises, but Lillian Jean isn't satisfied:

'That ain't enough. Get down in the road.'
I looked up at her. 'You crazy?'
'You can't watch where you going, get in the road. Maybe that way you won't be bumping into decent white folks with your nasty little self.'
This second insult was almost too much to bear. ...'I ain't nasty,' I said, properly holding my temper in check, 'and if you're so afraid of getting bumped, walk down there yourself.'

In these scenes, the different characters' attitudes are revealed through their actions and speech, from the arrogant contempt of the whites to Cassie's strong-willed assertiveness. As the novel progresses, Cassie learns more about the injustice and cruelty of the society in which she lives ● **see pp 60–62**. By the end of the book, when T.J., a black boy she has known all her life, is arrested for a murder he didn't do, she knows she won't see him again:

Come October, we would trudge to school as always, barefooted and grumbling, fighting the dust and the mud and the Jefferson Davis school bus. But T.J. never would again.

The author influences our response to Cassie and arouses sympathy for her by showing us events from her viewpoint and letting us share her feelings of bewilderment and injustice as she learns the hard way.

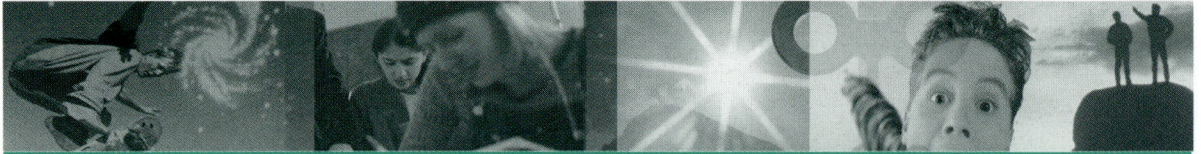

HIGHER PERFORMANCE

A way of presenting character used by some modern writers is a technique called 'stream of consciousness'. This aims to capture the flow of thoughts and impressions passing through a character's mind, from their viewpoint ▶ **see pp 32-40**. In *Moon Tiger* (1987), Penelope Lively shows how the mind of six-year-old Lisa works as she walks through a wood with her mother, Claudia:

The trees are singing. They also make whooshing and hissing noises and eyes stare from their trunks, shapes of big cruel eyes at which you must not look or creatures might pounce out and get you – ghosts and witches and old men like the old man who sweeps the street outside Claudia's house in London. If she can count to ten before she gets to the tree ... without going wrong nothing will get her, the horrid eyes will vanish; she does, and they do.

Here, the sound of the trees, the images prompted in Lisa's imagination and the connection with the old man in London are all shown in a flowing stream of associations. These are captured in one sentence, and given immediacy by use of the present tense.

If you're interested in seeing how other writers use this technique, you'll find James Joyce experimenting with it on the first page of *A Portrait of the Artist as a Young Man* (1916).

Quiz

1. What are some of the main methods used by writers to portray character?

2. What might be suggested about the following characters by their names?
a. Peter Pounce (*Joseph Andrews*)
b. Mr Gradgrind (*Hard Times*)
a. Heathcliff (*Wuthering Heights*)

3. How might we approach the study of characters who change?

4. How might your own response to a character change during a novel?

5. In the extracts from *Roll of Thunder, Hear My Cry*, how does the author engage our sympathy with Cassie?

Answers

1. Through physical appearance; choice of name; speech and actions; comments by other characters and by the author.

2. (i) 'Pounces' on other people's money! (ii) hard and unfeeling – worships facts; (iii) wild, with powers of endurance.

3. By focusing on their key experiences, and exploring how these affect the characters.

4. You might find you sympathise more or less with them; react with approval or disapproval.

5. By showing us events from her viewpoint so we share her feelings.

WHERE DOES THE STORY HAPPEN? – SETTING

Characters and environment

Atmosphere

Symbolism, feeling and theme

The setting is where and when a story takes place. An author may be interested in exploring the effect on characters of their environment, and perhaps how the characters try to change the conditions in which they live. Or the setting may be used for other purposes such as creating atmosphere, reflecting a character's emotions, or conveying themes.

KEY CONCEPTS

* Setting is the where and when of a story or novel

* Setting can reflect characters' emotions and convey themes, as well as being used realistically

* Symbolism is the use of something to represent or stand for something else

It can be tempting to skip what may look like boring bits of descriptive 'background'. However, such passages are often relevant, so we need to respond imaginatively to them.

When focusing on the setting, we can ask:

* Where and when are the key scenes set, and why?

* How does the author use detail to create our impression of the surroundings?

* How are characters affected, or acted on, by the setting? Do they act back on it?

* Does the setting reflect characters' feelings, or the book's themes? Is it being used symbolically?

The relationship between characters and their environment

Setting can refer to both physical surroundings and the society in which the characters live. For instance, Charles Dickens's *Hard Times* is set in the industrial north of England in the mid nineteenth century, when the appalling working conditions and exploitation of the workers by their masters led to social unrest.

William Golding's *Lord of the Flies* is set on an unpopulated tropical island during the Second World War; it is set on an island precisely because the author wants to show how, away from the rules of 'civilised' society, the boys regress into savagery, revealing the inherent destructiveness within human beings.

DID YOU KNOW?

Lord of the Flies echoes and explicitly refers to the setting in R.M. Ballantyne's adventure story, *The Coral Island* (1857). Through the contrast, William Golding is underlining his pessimistic vision of the evil in human nature.

Roll of Thunder, Hear My Cry

Mildred Taylor's *Roll of Thunder, Hear My Cry* is set in Mississippi in the American Deep South, in the 1930s. It depicts a society in which black people face racial discrimination, as well as severe economic hardship:

Two key features of the setting are: the school attended by the black children and the road along which they have to walk to school. Their school, 'a dismal end to an hour's journey', consists of:

> *four weather-beaten wooden houses on stilts of brick, 320 students, seven teachers, a principal, a caretaker, and the caretaker's cow, which kept the wide crabgrass lawn sufficiently clipped in spring and summer.*

The precise details here take on extra significance when contrasted with the description of the school attended by the white children, which is a 'long white wooden building' with 'a wide sports field' and an 'expansive front lawn'. There is also the detail of the flags:

> *In the very centre of the expansive front lawn, waving red, white and blue with the emblem of the Confederacy emblazoned in its upper left-hand corner, was the Mississippi flag. Directly below it was the American flag.*

THINK ABOUT IT

What significance do you see in the detail of the transposed flags?

The American flag should really be flying over the Mississippi flag. The fact that it isn't suggests the local whites' allegiance to the Southern tradition of white superiority (and slavery) under the Confederacy, rather than the principle of racial equality enshrined in the national constitution.

Mildred Taylor creates a picture of the schools through calling attention to significant details. She also does this in the description of the road along which the black children have to walk to school. On the first page, Cassie describes how, on the long walk, her six-year-old brother meticulously tries to keep himself clean, and how the Mississippi dust seems hostile to his efforts:

He lagged several feet behind ... attempting to keep the rusty Mississippi dust from swelling with each step and drifting back upon his shiny black shoes and the cuffs of his corduroy pants by lifting each foot high before setting it gently down again.

The road has steep banks on each side, and, depending on the weather, is very dusty or very muddy. When the white children's school bus passes, Cassie and her family have a daily hazard to face because the driver always showers them with dust or mud, to the amusement of the bus's jeering passengers. Cassie describes how, after rain, the dusty road 'churned into a fine red mud that oozed between our toes and slopped against our ankles as we marched miserably to and from school'. The description emphasises the struggle the blacks have, compared to the whites, to get themselves educated.

One day, the children are completely covered with mud by the bus, its occupants shouting cries of 'Nigger! Nigger! Mud eater!' They decide to get their own back. To avoid reprisals, they have to make this look like an accident. They secretly dig a trench in the road, which is hidden by flood water. When the bus returns, they watch from the shelter of the forest as it runs into the ditch and breaks down:

The bus ... rolled cautiously through a wide puddle some twenty feet ahead; then, seeming to grow bolder as it approached our man-made lake, it speeded up, spraying the water in high sheets of backward waterfalls into the forest ... but instead of the graceful glide through the puddle that its occupants were expecting, the bus emitted a tremendous crack and careered drunkenly into our trap.

Here we see how Mildred Taylor uses the setting to focus on key aspects of the struggle and discrimination that are part of the children's lives. In the novel as a whole, Cassie and her family aren't just acted on by their environment, they try to act back on it in various ways. The use of the setting in the road incident provides a small example of this, as the children actually change the setting by digging a ditch in it!

DID YOU KNOW?
Contrast between settings can be important. For example, Emily Brontë's *Wuthering Heights* alternates between the two houses of Wuthering Heights, with its wild moors, and the civilised Thrushcross Grange down in the valley. These two settings correspond with differences between the characters living in the houses, and contribute to the novel's themes ▶ see pp 22–31.

Other ways of using the setting

A writer may use the setting to create mood or atmosphere. In *The Return of the Native* (1878), Thomas Hardy's long description of the wild vastness of Egdon Heath which could 'intensify the opacity of a moonless midnight to a cause of shaking and dread', creates a feeling of foreboding, and of the insignificance of human beings.

Or a writer may reflect a character's feelings through the setting. Thomas Hardy does this in *Tess of the d'Urbervilles* (1891). When Tess has recovered from her seduction and the death of her baby, and is walking to another valley to make a fresh start, he describes a 'thyme-scented, bird-hatching morning in May' that corresponds with Tess's feelings of renewal:

Tess of the d'Urbervilles

Her hopes mingled with the sunshine ... which surrounded her as she bounded along against the soft south wind. She heard a pleasant voice in every breeze, and in every bird's note seemed to lurk a joy.

Later, when her fortunes have taken a turn for the worse after she has been deserted by her husband, she survives by working on a farm in a stony turnip-field. The women have to unearth the bottom halves of the turnips that haven't been eaten by the animals:

Every leaf of the vegetable having already been consumed, the whole field was in colour a desolate drab; it was a complexion without features, as if a face, from chin to brow, should be only an expanse of skin. ... It was so high a situation, this field, that the rain had no occasion to fall, but raced along horizontally upon the yelling wind, sticking into them like glass splinters till they were wet through.

THINK ABOUT IT

The name Thomas Hardy gives this farm is Flintcombe-Ash. What do you think this name is intended to imply about the place and about Tess's situation?

'Flint' suggests the stone-covered fields, and the hardness of Tess's life. 'Ash' suggests how her hopes (of her husband's return) have died like the ashes of a burnt out fire.

Here, as well as giving us a picture of the physical conditions of farm work, the description of the drab, cold landscape reflects Tess's feelings of desolation, and suggests her suffering at this stage of the novel. **So the setting may be used as a metaphor or symbol to suggest something beyond the mere physical scene.**

Used in this symbolic way, the setting may be a way of conveying a theme. An example of this is Alan Paton's story *The Waste Land**, set in South Africa during the period of apartheid.

The Waste Land

---

* From *Debbie Go Home*; (Jonathan Cape, 1961)

It is about a black man on his way home one night, who finds a gang of youths (also black) waiting to rob him. There is a convent nearby, but its door is barred. So he escapes by running through derelict waste land, a 'wilderness of wire and iron and the bodies of old cars':

Something caught him by the leg, and he brought his stick crashing down on it, but it was no man, only some knife-edged piece of iron. He was sobbing and out of breath, but he pushed on into the waste, while behind him they pushed on also, knocking against the old iron bodies and kicking against tins and buckets. He fell into some grotesque shape of wire; it was barbed and tore at his clothes and flesh.

In the darkness, he hits one of his pursuers with his stick and hides under an old lorry. When the other youths eventually give up the hunt and leave, he discovers he has killed his own son.

In this story, we are given a picture of the waste land as a dark 'wilderness'. The references to the 'bodies' of wrecked cars suggest a graveyard, and the 'knife-edged piece of iron' and barbed wire which rips the man's face suggest a war zone. Taking all the details into account, the waste land appears as not just a patch of derelict ground, but a symbol for a whole society. This land offers only a hostile, barren environment for young black men to grow up in; families break up and sons drift into crime. The convent, with its barred door, also contributes to the picture; its Christian values of love and forgiveness seem unavailable to redeem the waste land.

HIGHER PERFORMANCE

Writers of short stories have to work in a more economical way than novelists, so often use details of the setting very suggestively. Guy de Maupassant demonstrates this technique in *Vendetta**. Set in Corsica, the story is about a widow whose only son is murdered. Having no male relatives to carry out the traditional vendetta (revenge) against the murderer, she dedicates herself to the task, patiently training her dog to attack him. The story starts with a description of the houses of Bonifacio, where the old woman lives. They overlook the dangerous stretch of sea between Corsica and Sardinia. Which of the details in this opening strike you as likely to have some connection with the story to come?

Clinging to the rock, gazing down upon those deadly straits where scarcely a ship ventures, they look like the nests of birds of prey. The sea and the barren coast, stripped of all but a scanty covering of grass, are for ever harassed by a restless wind, which sweeps along the narrow funnel, ravaging the banks on either side. In all directions the black points of innumerable rocks jut out from the water, with trails of white foam streaming from them like torn shreds of linen, floating and fluttering on the surface of the waves.

In fact, all the details turn out to be significant. The imagery associated with the houses prepares us for the old woman herself becoming a kind of 'bird of prey'. The 'restless wind' is another apt image, anticipating her unrelenting obsession with revenge. The water foaming round the rocks like 'torn shreds of linen' is echoed later when the dog tears the murderer's throat to shreds. The setting suggests a cruel environment very much in keeping with the widow's revenge.

Next time you read a story, try deliberately focusing on the details of the setting, and see if they relate to the story's characters and themes.

---

* From *Modern Short Stories* by G. de Maupassant (1850–1893); trans. Marjorie Laurie, (Everyman, 1934).

Quiz

1. What is meant by the setting of a novel or story?

2. As well as being used to provide a realistic context for characters, what other uses might a writer make of the setting?

3. How does a writer create our impression of a setting?

4. In what sense can setting be used symbolically?

5. What should you try NOT to do when coming across a description of the setting?

Answers

1. Where and when the action takes place.

2. To create atmosphere; to reflect characters' feelings; to convey themes.

3. By the use of significant detail.

4. It can stand for something beyond itself (e.g. in the examples from *Tess of the D'Urbervilles* and *The Waste Land*).

5. Dismiss it as an irrelevant 'backdrop'!

HOW'S THE STORY TOLD? – LANGUAGE & STYLE

Language and action
Language and emotion
Dialogue and speech

Students often find a writer's use of language difficult to write about. They become interested in the events that are being described, and sometimes forget that the language that allows us to see these events isn't like a clear glass window that allows us to see something that is happening outside. **The language that writers choose does more than just enable us to see something, it also alters what we see.** The main thing to grasp here is that writers have choices; there's always another way of expressing something – another word or another way of putting the words together. **The way a writer uses words is what is meant by style.**

KEY CONCEPTS

❋ The purpose of a piece of writing influences its style

❋ Writers make choices about the words they use and their order

❋ Look at a writer's choice of language and the effect it achieves

When studying a writer's use of language, the first thing to think about is the purpose of the writing. For example, it may aim to convey a sense of place or create atmosphere; it may aim to describe action or develop suspense; it may try to convey a character's feelings or dramatise a relationship; it may satirise a character or aim to teach us something.

The purpose of the writing will dictate the kind of writing it is. So, for instance, we might have writing that could be classed as descriptive, or as narrative, or a piece of dialogue between characters, or a passage that is satirical or didactic.

Then, looking more closely and analytically at the language, we can focus on:

- **Vocabulary and imagery** – the writer's choice of words, including use of figurative language

- **Features of grammar** – such as sentence structure (syntax) and tenses (e.g. past or present)

- **Phonology** – the use of rhythm and sound

All the time, we are not just trying to spot features of language, we are considering their effect, how they contribute to a passage's meaning and impact.

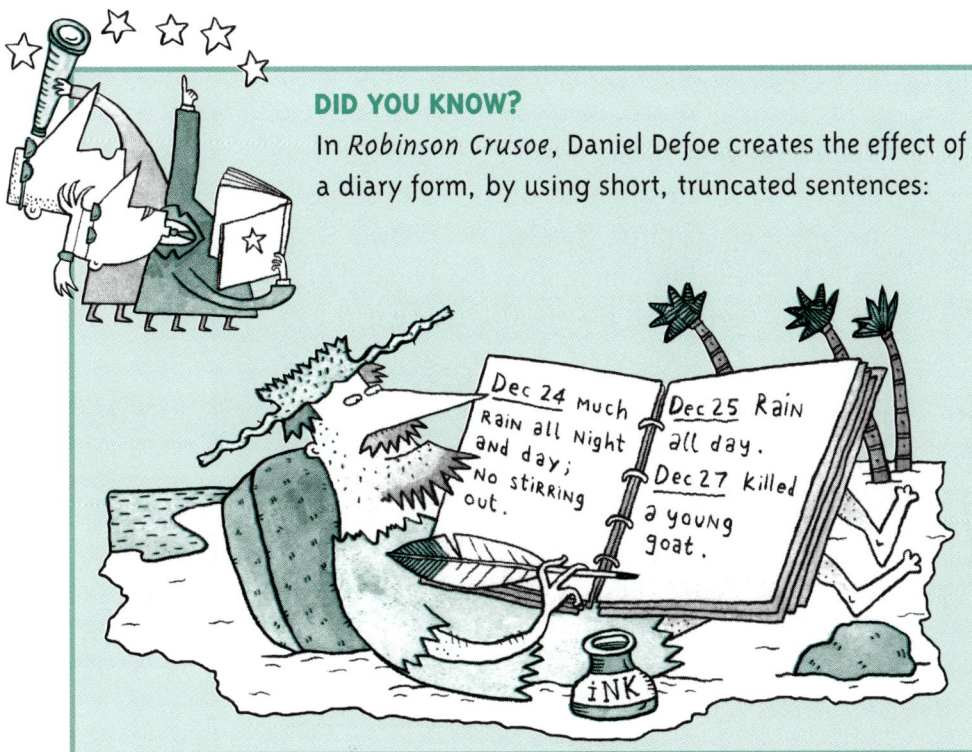

DID YOU KNOW?

In *Robinson Crusoe*, Daniel Defoe creates the effect of a diary form, by using short, truncated sentences:

We've already, inevitably, touched on the topic of language in earlier sections. For instance, we looked at the use of significant detail in relation to Setting ▶ **see pp 58–67**. And in the portrayal of Character ▶ **see pp 46–57** we came across the use of exaggeration for the purpose of satire, and of the present tense to convey the immediacy of a character's sensations. Here I should like to focus on the use of language:

- To describe action

- To convey a character's feelings

- To create dialogue

Use of language to describe action

DID YOU KNOW?

Ernest Hemingway was wounded on the Italian front in the First World War, involved in the Spanish Civil War, and a war correspondent in the Second World War. He tried to recreate action as vividly as possible and spoke of the difficulty of putting down 'what really happened in action; what the actual things were which produced the emotion that you experienced'.

The Short Happy Life of Francis Macomber

In Ernest Hemingway's story *The Short Happy Life of Francis Macomber* (1939), Macomber, an inexperienced American on safari in Africa, is hunting buffalo with a white hunter, Wilson. As they approach the animals in a car at 'a wild forty-five miles an hour', Hemingway shows us events through Macomber's eyes: 'the buffalo got bigger and bigger until he could see the grey, hairless, scabby look of one huge bull'. The description of the action continues in one very long sentence of over twenty lines. Here is part of it:

… they drew up close and he could see the plunging hugeness of the bull, and the dust in his sparsely haired hide, the wide boss of horn and his outstretched, wide-nostrilled muzzle …

The vocabulary is simple and precise with vivid visual details such as the close-up of the 'dust in the sparsely haired hide' and the 'wide-nostrilled muzzle'. The technical term 'boss' (bulge) suggests the world of big game hunting in which Macomber is a novice. The sentence continues:

… the brakes clamped on and the car skidded, ploughing sideways to an almost stop and Wilson was out on one side and he on the other, stumbling as his feet hit the still speeding-by of the earth, and then he was shooting at the bull as he moved away, hearing the bullets whunk into him, emptying his rifle at him as he moved steadily away, finally remembering to get his shots forward into the shoulder, and as he fumbled to re-load, he saw the bull go down.

KEY CONCEPTS

* ❋ Any striking use of words is worth exploring
* ❋ The length of a sentence, and the way it is put together can be expressive
* ❋ Sound and rhythm can emphasise the meaning of the words

One way to comment on a writer's use of language is to take words that strike you for any reason, and explore their effect. It can also help to replace these words with others of similar meaning, and see what difference it makes.

One striking use of language here is the way Macomber's feet are described as hitting 'the still speeding-by of the earth'. We wouldn't normally talk about someone's feet hitting a 'speeding-by'! We'd be more likely to say: 'his feet hit the earth which was still speeding by.' So Hemingway has chosen to break the normal rules of grammar according to which the verb 'hit' would normally be followed by a noun ('earth'). Writers sometimes deliberately break rules like this to achieve particular effects. Here, the effect is to convey Macomber's sense of not finding a solid object where he expects to find it, just the ground rushing by under his feet. This contributes to the excitement and confusion of being involved in the action.

We might also be struck by the word 'whunk', which isn't in my dictionary! Ernest Hemingway uses it for its sound, to mimic the distinctive, hollow thud of the bullet's moment of impact.

Finally, the length of the sentence itself provides a good illustration of how grammar can be expressive. The sentence describing the chase continues with no respite until the bull is 'downed', conveying the continuous action and speed of events.

Use of language to convey feeling

Jane Eyre

In *Jane Eyre* (1847), Jane's happy prospect of marrying Mr Rochester is smashed when she discovers he is already married. Charlotte Brontë conveys Jane's dazed feelings, making Jane tell her own story in the first person:

I was in my own room as usual – just myself, without obvious change: nothing had smitten me, or scathed me, or maimed me. And yet where was the Jane Eyre of yesterday? – where was her life? – where were her prospects?

Jane Eyre, who had been an ardent expectant woman – almost a bride – was a cold, solitary girl again: her life was pale; her prospects were desolate. A Christmas frost had come at midsummer; a white December storm had whirled over June; ice glazed the ripe apples, drifts crushed the blowing roses; on hayfield and cornfield lay a frozen shroud. … I looked on my cherished wishes, yesterday so blooming and glowing; they lay stark, chill, livid corpses that could never revive. I looked at my love … it shivered in my heart, like a suffering child in a cold cradle: sickness and anguish had seized it.

DID YOU KNOW?

In *Jane Eyre* Rochester claims his marriage isn't a proper one as his wife is mad. She is confined to the attic of Thornfield Hall and eventually starts a fire which burns it down. Jean Rhys created a character based on Rochester's mad first wife in *Wide Sargasso Sea*. But as she is the narrator for so much of the novel, we sympathise more with her view of events

▶ see p 32

In the third line, Jane refers to herself in the third person as if detached and numbed by the sudden change in her relationship. As the passage gets under way, she changes back to the first person as if the feelings start to belong to her. A series of metaphors, images of cold, winter and death convey her feelings of loss. Her hopes are likened to flowers turned into dead 'corpses' by a winter storm, destroyed before they can be fulfilled. The simile comparing her love to a sick child conveys her grief at what might have been had the love had a chance to grow. On the level of grammar, the repetition of phrases with a similar pattern ('A Christmas frost had come at midsummer; a white December storm had whirled over June ...'), results in a piling up of images of desolation that bury her under a feeling of despair. Reading the lines aloud, we can hear the insistent rhythm emphasising this feeling. Reading a text out loud will help you to be more aware of a writer's language and style.

NOTES

Use of dialogue

Another area where writers have a choice is when to use dialogue as opposed to summarising events. Dialogue involves direct speech, so we actually hear characters speaking. It's worth asking oneself what is gained by the use of dialogue at any particular point. Shortly after the above passage, Brontë uses dialogue as Jane describes how she refused Rochester's appeal to stay with him:

······································

'Jane, you understand what I want of you? Just this promise – "I will be yours, Mr Rochester."'

'Mr Rochester, I will not be yours.'

Another long silence.

'Jane!' recommended he, with a gentleness that broke me down with grief, and turned me stone-cold with ominous terror – for this still voice was the pant of a lion rising – 'Jane, do you mean to go one way in the world, and to let me go another?'

'I do.'

'Jane' (bending towards and embracing me), 'do you mean it now?'

'I do.'

'And now?' softly kissing my forehead and cheek.

'I do,' extricating myself from restraint rapidly and completely.

······································

Here, the author could have summarised the conversation by saying something like 'Despite everything he said, I still refused him.' Instead of this, she uses the language of direct speech. This allows her to dramatise the unfolding situation and involve the reader more closely in Jane's ordeal in which her love is in conflict with her principles. If we look at the characters' speech, we see Rochester tries to write Jane's script for her by putting the words 'I will be yours, Mr Rochester' into her mouth. However, she asserts her independence by repeating his words, at the same time reversing their meaning by adding 'not'. Her repetition of 'I do', to reject Rochester, shows her determination, but, in a cruelly ironic way, it echos the words she would have used to accept him in the previously interrupted wedding scene. The way the dialogue format makes the words stand out on the page emphasises this. So a sense of tension is created, as we feel that she would really like to be saying 'I do' in an accepting way, but can't.

Also of interest here, is that although Jane is narrating the event in the past tense, the dialogue is accompanied by bracketed stage directions from which the full form of the past tense is missing: '(bending towards and embracing me)'; 'softly kissing my forehead and cheek'. What do you feel the effect of this is? Does it add immediacy and suggest that the events are still happening for her?

DID YOU KNOW?

Jane Eyre was published in the Victorian period, a time when attitudes were more prudish than today. The novel was original for its time because it showed a good woman who was also capable of passion.

HIGHER PERFORMANCE

Some modern critics see novels as made up of a variety of different styles, 'voices' and dialects. It's worth looking at the different styles within a text and seeing what they contribute. For example, a writer may use dialect to suggest a character's regional origin or social class. In Thomas Hardy's *Tess of the d'Urbervilles*, Tess Durbeyfield lives in a rural peasant community with her family. Her feckless father, having learnt he is related to the aristocratic d'Urbervilles, has come home drunk. Tess's mother welcomes her home:

'Well, I'm glad you've come,' said her mother. ... 'I want to tell 'ee what have happened. Y'll be fess enough, my poppet, when th'st know!' (Mrs Durbeyfield habitually spoke the dialect; her daughter, who had passed the Sixth Standard in the National School ... spoke two languages: the dialect at home, more or less; ordinary English abroad and to persons of quality.)
'Since I've been away?' Tess asked.
'Ay!'
'Had it anything to do with father's making such a mommet of himself in thik carriage this afternoon? Why did 'er? I felt inclined to sink into the ground with shame!'

You will have noticed how Hardy intervenes here to comment on how Tess's speech, unlike her mother's, can shift in style as a result of her education. The fact that Tess is from a simple country family, but is more educated than her parents, contributes to Hardy's overall picture of the effects of change on country life in the last century, and to the tragedy that befalls Tess through her relationships with two men 'of quality'.

In *The Art of Fiction*, David Lodge comments:

'the language of the novel is not a language, but a medley of styles and voices'.

You might like to consider how many different 'styles and voices' you can find in any novel you are reading at the moment.

Quiz

1. What is style?

2. What is a useful foundation for analysing a writer's use of language?

3. Name three important areas of language use which can be considered in an analysis.

4. What is figurative language?

5. What is rhythm?

Answers

1. The way a writer uses language.

2. Consideration of the purpose of a piece of writing.

3. The choice of words; the writer's grammatical choices; sound and rhythm.

4. Language in which one thing is described in terms of another, which uses figures of speech (e.g. simile and metaphor).

5. The way the language moves.

THE STORY OF THE NOVEL

The eighteenth century
The nineteenth century
The twentieth century

Early days: the eighteenth century

In *Aspects of the Novel*, E.M. Forster reflects on the age-old appeal of stories:

> *Neanderthal man listened to stories, if one may judge by the shape of his skull. The primitive audience was an audience of shock-heads, gaping round the camp-fire, fatigued with contending against the mammoth or the woolly rhinoceros, and only kept awake by suspense. What would happen next?*

UGG WAZ ERE

Although human beings have told and listened to stories for thousands of years, **most people see the modern English novel emerging as a literary form in the eighteenth century** with the work of Daniel Defoe, Samuel Richardson and Henry Fielding.

DID YOU KNOW?

Daniel Defoe's *Robinson Crusoe* starts a tradition of stories about desert islands away from 'normal' civilised society. This leads down through R.M. Ballantyne's *The Coral Island* and R.L. Stevenson's *Treasure Island* (1883) to William Golding's *Lord of the Flies* and Aldous Huxley's *Island* (1962).

Because Richardson's novels (e.g. *Clarissa*, 1747-8) were in the form of letters (epistolary form) written by the characters, he could explore his character's psychology and inner feelings. Fielding's novels (e.g. *Joseph Andrews*, 1742) focused more on social satire than in-depth psychological exploration.

THINK ABOUT IT

Henry Fielding's sister, Sarah, also a writer, was interested, like Samuel Richardson, in what she called 'the inward turns of the mind'. Richardson praised her at her brother's expense: 'His was but as the knowledge of the outside of a clock-work machine, while yours was that of all the finer springs and movements of the inside.' (Letter to Sarah Fielding, 1756).

What was he saying?

Richardson and Fielding have been seen as founders of two different traditions in the English novel.

One tradition, that of focusing on the inner lives of characters can be found in the novels of such modern writers as Dorothy Richardson (e.g. *Pilgrimage*, The first volume of which appeared in 1915) and Virginia Woolf (e.g. *Mrs Dalloway*, 1925).

DID YOU KNOW?

A recent novel using the **epistolary form** (letters) is Alice Walker's *The Color Purple*.

The other tradition, of social satire, can be seen in such modern writers as Evelyn Waugh (*Decline and Fall*, 1928) and Kingsley Amis (*Lucky Jim*, 1954). In fact, **most authors combine elements of both approaches**, though the emphasis may well be on one or the other.

The eighteenth century also saw the birth of **Gothic novels** and stories, typically containing supernatural, gruesome and spooky events often set in graveyards, dungeons and ruined castles. It's interesting to try to connect changes in the way people thought and felt about the world in this period, with what they were interested in reading. At the risk of oversimplifying, readers seem to have reacted against the more rational, balanced approach to life in the first part of the eighteenth century and been attracted to books dealing with emotional extremes, violence, fantasy and the supernatural.

N
O
T
E
S

Early examples of Gothic novels include Horace Walpole's *The Castle of Otranto* (1764), Anne Radcliffe's *Mysteries of Udolpho* (1794) and Mary Shelley's *Frankenstein* (1818). Aspects of Gothic are parodied by Jane Austen in *Northanger Abbey* (1818), but go on appearing in the nineteenth century in the work of writers like Charles Dickens and the Brontë sisters. The influence of Gothic is still pervasive in the twentieth century, for example in the work of Mervyn Peake (e.g. *Gormenghast*, 1950) and Angela Carter (e.g. *The Magic Toyshop*, 1967), not to mention the horror fiction of writers like Stephen King, and of course modern horror films.

The nineteenth century

In the early nineteenth century, we again have a contrast
between two major figures: Jane Austen with her realistic
handling of everyday life (e.g. *Pride and Prejudice,* 1813) and
Sir Walter Scott, whose romantic historical novels (e.g.
Ivanhoe, 1819) were very influential.

The nineteenth century was a period of great social change.

Labelled 'the age of machinery' by Thomas Carlyle, it was a
time of rapid industrialisation and social inequality
accompanied by agitation for political reform. Social problems
were a popular theme, as in Charles Dickens's *Hard Times* and
Elizabeth Gaskell's *North and South* (1855), both of which
brought home the appalling working conditions in the
industrial North of England to middle-class readers in the
South.

More generally, **a common theme is the individual's struggle in an often hostile society.** This appears in Dickens's work and that of the Brontës, William Thackeray and George Eliot. Charlotte Brontë's heroines (e.g. *Jane Eyre*) are at odds with conventional society around them. Emily Brontë's Heathcliff (*Wuthering Heights*) is violently opposed to the society (represented by Thrushcross Grange and Wuthering Heights) which degrades him and takes away his love. William Thackeray (e.g. *Vanity Fair*, 1847) and Dickens (e.g. *Great Expectations*) both attack a society in which money and snobbery have become more important than human relationships. George Eliot (e.g. *Middlemarch*, 1871–2) explores society's effect on an individual's attempts to find fulfilment, and the extent to which an individual can in turn affect that society. In the late nineteenth century, the often tragic effects of change on people living in the country are portrayed in the novels of Thomas Hardy (e.g. *Tess of the d'Urbervilles*).

The short story

The nineteenth century is generally regarded as the period in which the modern short story began being taken seriously as an independent form.

THINK ABOUT IT

Is the short story just a truncated novel? Or has it features distinguishing it from the novel?

Look at its concentration and economy; its reliance even more than the novel on suggestive detail; its tendency to focus on a moment of crisis in a character's life.

From the start, stories involving horror, ghosts and the supernatural were popular. Three writers who were very influential in the later development of the short story were the American Edgar Allan Poe, the Russian Anton Chekhov and the Frenchman Guy de Maupassant. Poe excelled in writing horror stories like *The Pit and the Pendulum* (1843) and detective stories like *The Murders in the Rue Morgue* (1841). The realism and directness of Maupassant's stories, published in the 1880s, with their strong plots often with a twist in the tail like *The Necklace*, influenced Rudyard Kipling. Chekhov's stories, such as *The Lady with the Little Dog* (1899), with their suggestive use of detail, influenced writers like Katherine Mansfield.

KEY CONCEPTS

❋ The novel is a relatively recent literary form

❋ Over time new subject matters and techniques have emerged

❋ The novel has been influenced by changes in society and ways of seeing the world

NOTES

The twentieth century

The twentieth century sees new areas of experience chosen as subject matter, and developments in technique based on a changing view of the world. One trend has been the tendency to avoid using the technique of narration by an all-knowing author, owing to a decline in confidence in there being one 'true' version of reality. Instead, **events may be portrayed through the consciousness of someone who doesn't know all the facts** and is themselves trying to make sense of things. Henry James used this approach, as did Joseph Conrad whose *Lord Jim* (1900) and *Heart of Darkness* (1902) have a narrator called Marlow who is himself trying to understand the characters he tells us about.

The importance attached by modern writers to the unconscious, to dreams, fantasy and early childhood experience, is partly due to the influence of Sigmund Freud, the founder of psychoanalysis. It is reflected in the **'stream of consciousness'** technique practised by writers such as James Joyce (e.g. *Ulysses*, 1922) and Virginia Woolf (e.g. *Mrs Dalloway*), and in the interest of writers like D.H. Lawrence (e.g. *The Rainbow*) in the unconscious and instinctual life of his characters.

The use of non-chronological plots in modern fiction is partly a reflection of a way of thinking about the nature of time that differs from the traditional way of seeing it as a matter of straightforward linear progression. Some modern writers have focused on how we experience time subjectively: for example, in William Golding's *Pincher Martin* (1956) the last few seconds of a drowning man's life, in which he relives past experiences, are expanded into a whole novel.

In the 1950s some people claimed the novel was 'dead'. You only have to go into a bookshop to see that despite television, videos and computers, the novel and short story are still alive and well. Take as an example the enormous success of Louis de Bernière's *Captain Corelli's Mandolin* (1994), which has, to date, sold well in excess of a million copies. There was little advertising for it when it was published. A few people bought it, loved it and recommended it to their friends. The friends recommended it to their friends, and news soon spread that it was a terrific read.

Similarly, huge sales of novels such as *Birdsong* (1997) by Sebastian Faulks, *Angela's Ashes* (1996) by Frank McCourt and Vikram Seth's *A Suitable Boy* (1994) all show that the novel is as alive as it ever has been.

A final development that must be mentioned, however, is the **tremendous wealth of fiction by writers in other countries where English is spoken**. This applies not just to America, Canada and Australia, but to countries which have more recently become independent from colonial rule, such as India, Africa and the West Indies. Writers like Anita Desai (e.g. *The Village by the Sea*), Chinua Achebe (e.g. *Things Fall Apart*) and Michael Anthony (e.g. *Green Days by the River*, 1967) (to name but a few) can **give a reader access to the experience of another culture that they might otherwise never have had.**

Extending one's experience of the world in this way is one of the reasons people engage in what may seem the strange activity of reading fiction. Strange, in that something that isn't literally true can so absorb people, make them aware of different possibilities in life, and give them fuller understanding of themselves.

Ernest Hemingway commented on this paradox:

....
All good books have one thing in common – they are truer than if they had really happened, and after you've read one of them you will feel that all that happened, happened to you and then it belongs to you for ever.
....

I hope you agree!

Ten Great Reads

Here are ten contemporary novels, chosen at random and all excellent, which are likely to become classics of the twentieth century. Read them and enjoy!

Captain Corelli's Mandolin by Louis de Bernières

Birdsong by Sebastian Faulks

Possession by A.S. Byatt

A Suitable Boy by Vikram Seth

Enduring Love by Ian McEwan

Angela's Ashes by Frank McCourt

Sophie's World by Jostein Gaarder

Regeneration by Pat Barker

Bridget Jones's Diary by Helen Fielding

Alias Grace by Margaret Atwood

Story, Plot, Narrative Structure

1. Is the following a narrative? (Give your reasons):

   Eagles (part of family Accipitridae). They are large, broad-winged birds of prey with large heads and bills. ... Most eagles are scarce in numbers owing to persecution, the effect of poisonous chemicals and a slow reproduction rate. Nest singly, far from human habitation.

2. In *Life of Ma Parker** (1922), by Katherine Mansfield, Ma Parker is a cleaning-woman who has had a very hard life. Yesterday, she attended the funeral of her much-loved little grandson. Today she is cleaning her employer's house:

   She took her brushes and cloths into the bedroom. But when she began to make the bed, smoothing, tucking, patting, the thought of little Lennie was unbearable. Why did he have to suffer so? That's what she couldn't understand.

   ... From Lennie's little box of a chest there came a sound as though something was boiling. There was a great lump of something bubbling in his chest that he couldn't get rid of. When he coughed the sweat sprang out on his head; his eyes bulged, his hands waved, and the great lump bubbled as a potato knocks in a saucepan.

   In terms of narrative structure, what technique is Katherine Mansfield using here? What is its effect?

Answers

1. This isn't a narrative. It doesn't contain a series of events.
2. Flashback. It shows Ma Parker reliving her grandson's suffering.

---

* From *The Garden Party and Other Stories*; (Penguin, 1951)

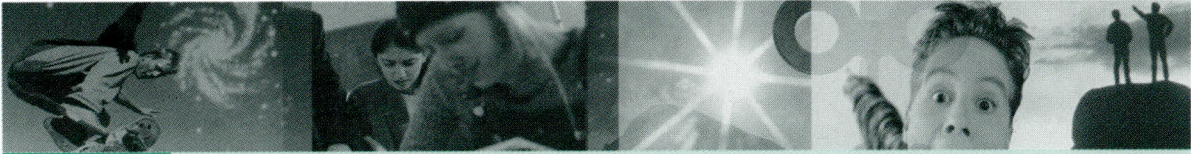

Theme

1. With which of the following statements do you agree?

    a. A text has one correct interpretation. You will lose marks in an exam if you don't get it right.

    b. A text can have alternative interpretations. You will get credit in an exam for putting forward an interpretation that is supported by evidence.

2. How would you describe the theme of the extract on page 90 from *Life of Ma Parker*?
    You might like to go on to link your sense of what the passage is about to features of the author's style. What do you notice about the way the text is written that contributes to its effect?

Answers

1. (b) is true.
2. I would say that the extract is about loss, grief and the response to suffering. The use of the flashback shows that despite Ma Parker's present involvement in the repetitive business of housework ('smoothing, tucking, patting'), the vivid memory of her grandson irresistibly intrudes to remind her of her loss. There are graphic physical details that allow us to see and hear the boy in his last illness. These include the horrifying image (a domestic one that would come naturally to Ma Parker) of the lump bubbling and knocking in his chest like a potato on the boil. This focuses on both the child's suffering, and the pain caused to his grandmother as she rewitnesses it. There is something homely and comforting about the idea of a potato on the boil, but the fact that here it is incongruously associated with a child's suffering helps to capture Ma Parker's sense of wrongness and bafflement.

Viewpoint and Voice

1. In the extract from *Life of Ma Parker* (p.90) from whose viewpoint is the story told? Why do you think the writer has chosen this viewpoint?

2. From Henry Fielding's *Joseph Andrews*, here is a description of Mrs Slipslop who fancies the handsome (and considerably younger) hero, Joseph:

   She was not at this time remarkably handsome; being very short, and rather too corpulent in body, and somewhat red, with the addition of pimples in the face. Her nose was likewise rather too large, and her eyes too little; nor did she resemble a cow so much in her breath as in two brown globes which she carried before her; one of her legs was also a little shorter than the other, which occasioned her to limp as she walked. This fair creature had long cast the eyes of affection on Joseph, in which she had not met with quite so good success as she probably wished.

   How would you describe the tone of the author's voice here? How does it influence your response to Mrs Slipslop?

Answers

1. Ma Parker's. To engage our sympathy with her.
2. You might describe the tone as humorous, satirical or ironic. A humorous effect is achieved by exaggerating Mrs Slipslop's unattractiveness alongside the understatement that she was 'not at this time remarkably handsome'. Calling her a 'fair creature' is blatantly ironic. She acts as if she were 'fair' but is depicted as the opposite. As readers, therefore, we may laugh at her vanity and illusions.

Character

In Charlotte Brontë's *Jane Eyre*, Mr Brocklehurst runs a boarding school to which ten-year-old Jane is being sent by her guardian Mrs Reed. Here, Jane tells of her first meeting with him. Mrs Reed has just commented disapprovingly (and unjustly) on Jane's behaviour, Mr Brocklehurst replies:

'Sorry indeed to hear it! She and I must have some talk'; and bending from the perpendicular, he installed his person in the arm-chair, opposite Mrs Reed's. 'Come here,' he said.

I stepped across the rug: he placed me square and straight before him. What a face he had, now that it was almost on a level with mine! what a great nose! and what a mouth! and what large, prominent teeth!

'No sight so sad as that of a naughty child,' he began, 'especially a naughty little girl. Do you know where the wicked go after death?'

'They go to hell,' was my ready and orthodox answer.

'And what is hell? Can you tell me that?'

'A pit full of fire.'

'And should you like to fall into that pit, and to be burning there for ever?'

1. What impression do you form of Mr Brocklehurst?

2. What methods are being used to portray him?

Answers

1. Mr Brocklehurst is portrayed as a self-important prig who has no sympathy with children.

2. You could show how this is done through exploring the effect of his appearance, his actions and his speech. His name also has a rather pompous ring to it. As Jane is the narrator, we are also influenced by her view of him. The language with which she describes how he 'installed his person in the arm-chair' suggests his self-importance.

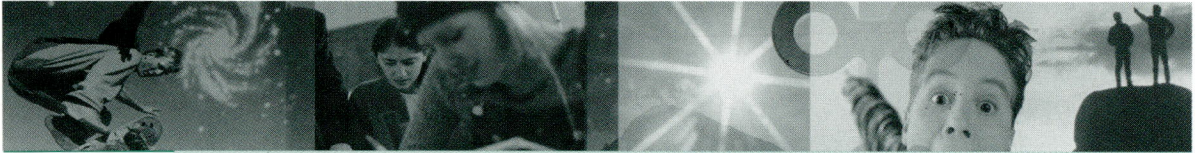

Setting

1. 'The setting of a novel or story isn't that important; we should concentrate on the characters and themes.'
True or false?

2. In this extract from Emily Brontë's *Wuthering Heights*, the narrator, Nelly, describes how Heathcliff has just run away having overheard Cathy say it would degrade her to marry him. When Cathy discovers this, she is distraught and rushes outside despite an approaching storm to find him. How is the setting being used here?

It was a very dark evening for summer: the clouds appeared inclined to thunder. ... Catherine would not be persuaded into tranquillity. She kept wandering to and fro ... in a state of great agitation ... and at length took up a permanent position on one side of the wall, near the road: where, heedless of ... the growling thunder and the great drops that began to plash around her, she remained, calling at intervals and then listening, and then crying outright. ... About midnight, while we still sat up, the storm came rattling over the Heights in full fury. There was a violent wind, as well as thunder, and either one or the other split a tree off at the corner of the building.

Answers

1. False. The setting may tell us things about the characters and themes.
2. A threatening atmosphere is created. It is unusually dark and the thunder is described as 'growling' like a dangerous animal. This reflects the ominous nature of the incident that has just occurred, suggesting its fateful consequences and foreshadowing Heathcliff's vengeful return. The violence of the elements also **reflects the violence of Cathy's emotions.**

Did you get it?

Language and Style

1. The linguist Michael Halliday has said: 'Language is as it is because of what it has to do.'
   How do you think this applies to analysing a writer's style and use of language?

2. Here is a description of a horse-race from Ernest Hemingway's *My Old Man* (1923).

   a. What is the purpose of the writing? (To use Halliday's terms, what has the language to do?)

   b. How is language being used to achieve that purpose (or do what it has to do)?

   ....

   War Cloud came on faster than I'd ever seen anything in my life and pulled up on Foxless that was going fast as any black horse could go with the jock flogging hell out of him with the gad and they were right dead neck for a second but War Cloud seemed going about twice as fast with those great jumps and that head out – but it was while they were neck and neck that they passed the winning post and when the numbers went up in the slots the first one was 2 and that meant that Foxless had won.

   ....

Answers

1. Analysis needs to be based on looking at the purpose of the writing, on what the language has to do.
2. a. Perhaps the main purpose is to give an impression of the speed of a horse-race and the narrator's emotional involvement.
   b. This is achieved through the use of one long sentence that races along like the horses until the finishing post. Colloquial language (e.g. 'flogging hell out of him') gives the impression of someone speaking excitedly.

Index